insight text guide

Avril Good

# The Memory Police

Yōko Ogawa

First published in 2023, reprinted in 2024, 2025.

Insight Publications Pty Ltd
3/350 Charman Road
Cheltenham VIC 3192
Australia
Tel: +61 3 8571 4950
Email: books@insightpublications.com.au

**www.insightpublications.com.au**

A catalogue record for this book is available from the National Library of Australia

*Yōko Ogawa's The Memory Police* / Avril Good

Avril Good asserts the moral right to be identified as the author of this work.

ISBNs:
9781922771780 (print)
9781922771797 (digital)

Cover design by Melisa Paredes

Proudly printed in Australia by Ligare Book Printers

# contents

# CHARACTER MAP

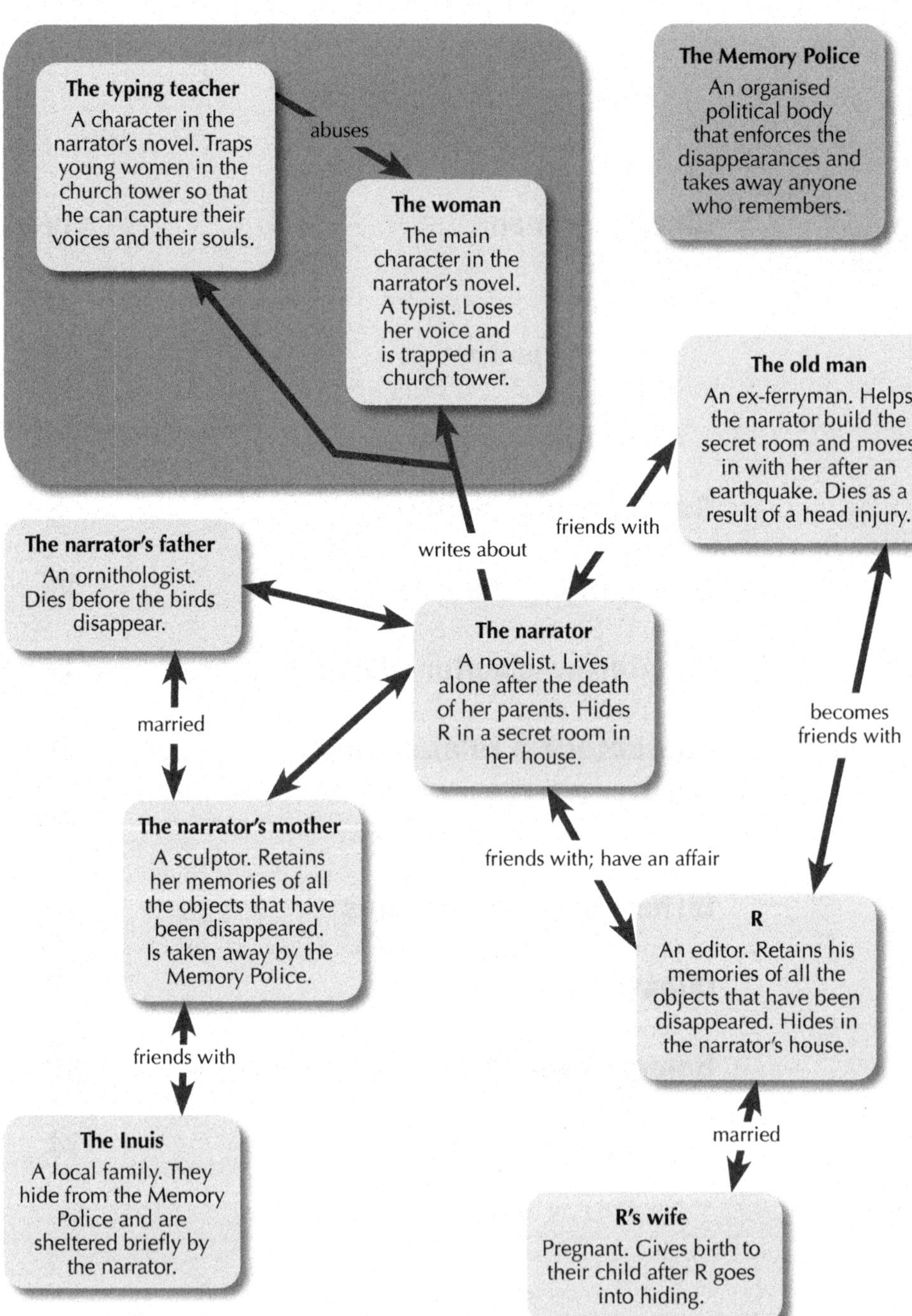

# OVERVIEW

## About the author

Yōko Ogawa, born in 1962, has won every major Japanese literary award. Her work was first published in 1988, and since then she has published more than forty works of fiction and nonfiction, only some of which have been translated into English. Her most well-known works that have been published in English include *The Diving Pool* (2008), *Hotel Iris* (2010) and *The Housekeeper and the Professor* (2009), the last two of which have been adapted into films.

Ogawa writes about characters who live in the margins of society. In an interview with Itakura Kimie, she discusses this recurring device in her works:

> In my novels, there are lots of characters who find it hard to live in society due to something they lack. Maybe I was influenced by encountering so many people like that when I was a child. They've been swept into a corner, where they seem to live on the verge of being swallowed up by the darkness. (quoted in Kimie 2020)

Ogawa's writing is often concerned with the human body, as well as femininity, violence and power. Eric Margolis writes that 'Ogawa tells stories about gender power dynamics and women struggling to break free from the control of men … She masterfully executes her signature literary form – a form of surrealism where metaphor becomes reality' (Margolis 2020).

Ogawa lives in Ashiya, Japan with her husband and son.

## Synopsis

On an unnamed island, objects are disappeared. A disappeared object loses its meaning and cannot be remembered by the inhabitants of the island. Any references to such objects are destroyed by the Memory Police, who are tasked with enforcing these disappearances.

The narrator lives alone after the death of her parents. It is suggested that the Memory Police may have been instrumental in the death of the narrator's mother, given that she had the ability to remember the disappeared objects. Her father, however, died of natural causes. He had studied birds, and the narrator holds fond memories of bird watching with him when she would visit his office. Five years following his death, birds are disappeared and the Memory Police visit to destroy all images and references to birds in the narrator's house.

As a writer, the narrator pens stories of loss, heavily influenced by the disappearances in her daily life. She is friends with an old man, with whom she shares her novels, and R, her editor. When R reveals his ability to remember, the narrator, with the help of the old man, devises a plan to hide R within her home as she knows he is in danger of arrest by the Memory Police. R agrees, although it means leaving behind his wife and unborn child.

The old man is taken by the Memory Police and interrogated regarding a boatful of people who escaped the island. As a former ferry mechanic, he is under suspicion of helping them. The narrator visits the headquarters of the Memory Police in the hopes of finding information about the old man, but she is herself questioned. The old man is released three days later.

R's wife has her baby, and R, the old man and the narrator celebrate the old man's birthday. Their celebration is interrupted by a visit from the Memory Police who fortunately do not discover the hidden room. Later that night, R and the narrator kiss and thereafter spend many nights together. On the island, items continue to disappear: roses, photographs and, eventually, novels. The citizens of the island burn all the books but, at R's insistence, the narrator continues to write in secret.

The island is further traumatised by an earthquake that injures the old man, causing lethal damage that does not become apparent until later. The narrator and the old man find and preserve disappeared objects hidden in sculptures made by the narrator's mother. R believes that interacting with these objects will restore their memories, but the narrator and the old man struggle to find any meaning in the objects.

The old man dies from his injuries, leaving the protagonist and R alone. Despite her grief, the narrator finishes her manuscript. The novel she is writing is recounted, in stages, in *The Memory Police*. The story is that of a woman, imprisoned in the clock tower of a church by her typing teacher, who was formerly her lover. He has trapped her voice in a typewriter, which subsequently breaks, rendering her voiceless. The woman slowly loses all sense of hope, feeling as though she exists only for the typing teacher, and begins to lose her sight. Eventually, as the typing teacher brings a new girl to the tower, the woman is absorbed into the room, symbolising the erasure of her identity.

The narrator herself faces a similar fate as the disappearances extend to legs, arms and then entire bodies. Eventually, the narrator is left with only her voice and seeks comfort from R in his hidden room. She expresses hope that she will be remembered, and as she disappears entirely, R emerges into the outside world.

## Character summaries

### The narrator

The unnamed narrator is a novelist who has lost both her parents. She lives alone, but is close friends with an old man. Like most of the inhabitants of the island, the narrator cannot remember the disappeared objects. Initially accepting of the disappearances, her friendship with her editor, R – who is able to remember – makes her see the necessity of resisting. She hides R in a secret room in her house. By the end of the novel, the narrator has lost her sense of self, as well as her entire body, and is left to disappear in the hidden room.

### The Memory Police

The Memory Police are a mysterious force who uphold the disappearances. They act with efficiency and cruelty as they seek to destroy any references to disappeared objects, and to hunt down anyone who retains their memories. It is not known whether they control the disappearances, or merely take advantage of them to consolidate their power on the island. They act as one body, lacking in individual identity.

### R

R is an editor. He is married, and during the course of the novel, his wife gives birth to their child. Unlike most of the characters in the text, R retains his memories, making him a target for the Memory Police. He hides in a secret room in the narrator's house, becoming increasingly isolated from the outside world. He encourages his friends – the narrator and the old man – to resist the disappearances, as he believes they are destroying their souls. At the end of the novel, R leaves the hidden room and re-enters the outside world.

### The old man

The old man was once a mechanic on the ferry that previously linked the island with other places, and now lives on his non-functional boat. He, like the narrator, forgets the disappeared objects. He is resigned to these disappearances and frequently encourages the narrator not to worry about them. The old man helps to hide R and carries out other small acts of resistance, such as delivering messages to R's wife. His boat is damaged in an earthquake, in which he also sustains injuries that eventually lead to his death.

### The woman

The woman in the narrator's novel is a typing student. She becomes trapped in the clock tower of a church after her lover and teacher locks her voice in a typewriter. When the typewriter breaks, she loses her voice, then gradually her sight and, eventually, all sense of self. She cannot even bring herself to escape from the tower when an opportunity arises. The woman is eventually absorbed into the tower room.

### The typing teacher

The typing teacher is a character in the narrator's novel who imprisons some of his students in a tower room and steals their voices. His current victim is the woman. He is cold and cruel, seeking to control every aspect of the woman's body and identity. His pattern of abuse is made apparent when he loses interest in the woman and brings a new girl to the tower.

# BACKGROUND & CONTEXT

## Historical context

Yōko Ogawa's novel draws extensively from the context of World War II and Nazi Germany's systemic persecution of Jewish people. The genocide of six million Jewish people by the Nazis is now referred to as the Holocaust. The horror of the Holocaust has left an indelible mark on the human consciousness and Jewish people today still suffer from intergenerational trauma as a result of these atrocities.

Some Jewish people used false identities and passed themselves off as non-Jewish to escape persecution. Many Jewish people were unable to use such methods and instead hid in places such as cellars, attics, barns or even caves. Hiding in this way required support from others, so that food and other necessities could be obtained. But this carried the risk of denunciation from friends or other members of the community who might notice.

Ogawa's novel takes inspiration from the heart-wrenching tale of Anne Frank, a Jewish girl forced into hiding during the Holocaust. Anne Frank's *Diary of a Young Girl* (1947) detailed her life in hiding and became a symbol of the lost potential of the children killed in the Holocaust. *The Memory Police* is heavily influenced by Anne Frank's personal narrative, which Ogawa read as a teenager.

> Anne's heart and mind were so rich … Her diary proved that people can grow even in such a confined situation. And writing could give people freedom … I wanted to digest Anne's experience in my own way and then recompose it into my work. (quoted in Rich 2019)

The correlation between the texts is most evident in the dynamic between the narrator and her editor, R, who is secreted away in a hidden room. This image evokes the haunting memory of the secret annexe where Anne Frank and her family concealed themselves for two years, hidden behind a bookcase in the building where Anne's father had his business. Other stories of hiding and rescue during the Holocaust resonate within the pages of *The Memory Police*, such as that of the Ulma family who, despite the threat of death, sheltered Polish Jewish families. Even after the members of the Ulma family were murdered for their actions, their neighbours continued to shelter Jewish families until the end of the war.

Japan's involvement in World War II was characterised by censorship and the denial of its wartime atrocities. One of the most significant examples is the Nanjing Massacre, also called the Rape of Nanjing, when hundreds of thousands of Chinese citizens were slaughtered and subjected to rape, brutality and other horrors as ordered by the Imperial Japanese Army. Textbook censorship and government denials mean Japanese citizens have not always been made aware of historical events such as this. Like in *The Memory Police*, there has been a collective forgetting.

> Even today, there is heated nationalistic grandstanding from some quarters about the historical legitimacy of 'comfort women', young women and girls from colonized countries who were forced into sexual slavery by the Japanese Imperial Army, the majority of whom were from Korea and China. The discussions regarding official state apologies and reparations for these and other atrocities have reappeared as recently as January 2021. There are so many intentional gaps in Japanese history regarding WWII that many Japanese citizens aren't even aware of these events. Or these historical facts are painted as propaganda pushed by enemies of the Japanese state and shouldn't be believed. (Shiota 2021)

## Political context

The political landscape of the twentieth century was marked by the rise and fall of totalitarian regimes. *The Memory Police* is set against the backdrop of an anonymous police state, alluding to the broader political context of authoritarian regimes. The titular Memory Police bear a stark resemblance to secret police agencies such as the Gestapo in Nazi Germany and the KGB in the Soviet Union, infamous for their brutal methods of ensuring state control.

Authoritarian governments are characterised by a central power that limits and controls the political freedoms, rights and civil liberties of their citizens. They often employ strategies such as surveillance, brainwashing and force to enact their regimes, and will discriminate against and persecute those who dissent.

In Ogawa's novel, the citizens' acceptance of the ongoing disappearances can be seen as an allegorical representation of 'the banality of evil'. This is a concept coined by political theorist Hannah Arendt during the trial of Adolf Eichmann, a major organiser of the Holocaust. According to Arendt, Eichmann was not driven by an inherent evil, but by an unthinking adherence to the Nazi regime (Aharony 2010).

In a similar sense, the citizens of the island unquestioningly obey the authoritarian regime of the Memory Police. They are not depicted as evil figures, but their complicity in the erasure of memories is instrumental in ensuring that the government's control is effective. Essentially, the Memory Police are able to enforce their power and control because their methods are accepted by the general population as ordinary and just how things are.

## Publishing context

*The Memory Police* is a novel in translation. Originally published in Japan in 1994, it wasn't until 2019 that it was translated into English by

Stephen Snyder. Novels in translation often owe as much to the translator as to the original author, and though you should refer to Ogawa as the author of this text, it is important to remember that Snyder would have needed to make important language and editorial choices when translating that may have slightly altered the original tone or meaning.

In reflecting on the most challenging element of translating *The Memory Police*, Snyder reported:

> *The Memory Police* is a powerful, suspenseful novel, but it is also a quiet, meditative book full of moments of great beauty. The greatest challenge was to find the language and tone in English that communicated this complex combination of moods and styles that is so central to the original Japanese. Yoko Ogawa's prose in Japanese is extraordinarily beautiful, so it's always a challenge to try to find a way to capture even a vague sense of that beauty in English. (quoted in ShelfMedia 2020)

## Japanese culture

As Ogawa is a Japanese novelist, it is useful to consider how elements of Japanese culture may have influenced her text. References to Japanese food such as *ramune* and objects such as the *orugōru* are symbols in the novel for lost cultural heritage. There are references, too, to the household altar, a typical feature in many Japanese homes.

Many of the citizens of the island in Ogawa's text – particularly the old man – reflect the Japanese cultural ethos of *shikata ga nai*. This expression translates as 'it can't be helped' and shares a similar meaning to the French saying *c'est la vie*. It has been used as a response to wartime atrocities and implies that suffering should be endured because sometimes these circumstances are unavoidable. In this way, the attitude of *shikata ga nai* may have negative connotations for some, who view this endurance as complacency or a fatalistic acceptance of one's fate.

# GENRE, STRUCTURE & LANGUAGE

## Genre

Following the lead of classics such as George Orwell's *1984* (1949) and Margaret Atwood's *The Handmaid's Tale* (1985), *The Memory Police* is a dystopian novel. Dystopian texts are usually written to echo or magnify real-world issues and problems, and to present a worst-case scenario in order to warn readers of their dangers.

### Elements of a dystopia

Dystopian texts often include authoritarian governments who 'use illegitimate coercion like force, threats and the "disappearing" of dissidents to stay in power' (Atchison and Shames 2020). Dystopias in film, novels and television may also feature:

- a sense of fear
- surveillance and a lack of privacy
- loss of individualism
- manipulation of reality
- limits and infringements on individuals' rights
- extreme social hierarchies
- repression of emotion and desires.

## Structure

*The Memory Police* uses a traditional narrative structure: exposition, rising action, climax, falling action and resolution. The tragic ending of the novel is foreshadowed by the increasing horror of the disappearances, creating a sense of inevitability that, like the objects, the characters themselves will disappear. It is written using first-person point of view and follows the narrator's thoughts and feelings to allow readers to feel a sense of connection with the protagonist.

### Embedded narrative

Woven throughout *The Memory Police* is an embedded narrative – or story within a story – of the woman and the typing teacher. This embedded narrative is the narrator's novel, and the transitions back to the main story often include the narrator reflecting on what she has written. Formatting features clearly signify the shift to the embedded narrative, with the font changing to something resembling a typewriter font. The embedded narrative always begins a chapter and, except for the final section of this secondary story, is followed by a dinkus to denote the shift back to the main story.

## Language

Ogawa's language is minimalistic and detached, creating a sense of distance between the narrator and the reader. This distance is emphasised by Ogawa's decision not to name any of the protagonists or indeed even the island itself. Characters exist as single letters (R), as their connection to others (R's wife), as their occupation (the hatmaker) or as their age (the old man, the boy). In a world where meaning is gradually disappearing, the meaning we might attach to names is also not available to us.

This distancing effect can also be seen at a syntactical level in Ogawa's text. The opening sentence of the novel, 'I sometimes wonder what was disappeared first—among all the things that have vanished from the island' (p.3), uses the passive voice but also uses 'disappeared' as a transitive verb, which is an unusual grammatical choice and unsettles the reader from the very beginning.

### Description

Objects, before and after they disappear, are described with detail and attention to highlight their materiality and meaning. Ogawa also often uses personification to reveal the importance of objects, suggesting that they are living things and that their disappearance is a type of death. She also likens objects to natural elements and suggests that they can exert a powerful emotional pull on people. Examples of her detailed descriptions of objects include the following.

- 'The objects in my palm seemed to cower there, absolutely still, like little animals in hibernation, sending me no signal at all.' (p.5)
- 'The nails were soft and transparent, and came away with the least effort, fluttering to the floor like flower petals.' (p.39)
- 'I imagine [your heart] fitting perfectly in my palms, soft and slippery, like gelatin that hasn't quite set. It might wobble at the slightest touch, but I sense I'd need to hold it carefully, so it wouldn't slip through my fingers.' (p.82)
- 'The box was stained a dark brown and carved with a geometric pattern of diamond shapes … A blue glass bead was set in the lid, which was attached with small hinges, and the color seemed to change as the angle of the light shifted. The design wasn't particularly unusual, but something about the look of it made you want to hold it in your hand and open the lid.' (pp.143–4)
- '… the objects we had taken must have been shocked when we pulled them out into the world. I could almost sense their fear, coming through the bags.' (p.224)

In contrast, the Memory Police are dehumanised through the language used to describe them. Their machine-like actions and lack of individuality separate them from the ordinary citizens. Consider the following examples.

- 'They worked in silence, their eyes fixed, making no unnecessary movements.' (p.13)
- '… none of the men appeared to be sweating or suffering from the heat in any way.' (p.14)
- '… the forceful, rhythmic boots of the Memory Police …' (p.21)
- 'They're lurking everywhere …' (p.25)
- 'They stood as always, weapons on their hips, faces devoid of expression.' (p.47)

Ogawa also emphasises their violence and brutality through the language used to describe their actions, such as in the following examples.

- 'They invaded houses …' (p.64)
- 'They dragged out anyone they found …' (p.64)
- '… the Memory Police are out there hunting.' (p.109)
- '… the leader of the group … barked his question.' (p.150)
- '… the light glinting cruelly off their guns.' (p.155)
- '… the Memory Police forced them into the covered back of one of the trucks.' (p.155)

### Imagery

The metaphor of a swamp is often used to describe the narrator's memories, and water imagery more generally is used throughout the novel. The narrator alludes to 'the very bottom of [her] mind's swamp, the place where memories come to rest' (p.232). This metaphorical image becomes increasingly disturbing as the number of disappearances increases, which can be seen in the following quote:

> One after another, he tossed pebbles into the swamp of my mind, but instead of coming to rest on the bottom, they continued to drift deeper and deeper down without end. (pp.269–70)

This imagery evokes ideas about stagnation and stillness. Swamps have a negative connotation and, as they are places that are difficult to move through, are associated with entrapment. Through this metaphor, the narrator portrays her thoughts and memories as being stuck and beyond reach.

### Symbolism

*The Memory Police* imbues meaning into objects and seasons, giving the text a fable- or fairytale-like quality.

- *Snow*: Signals the end of hope. It is a relentless symbol of winter, covering the ground so completely that 'it was almost frightening to disturb it' (p.118) and its constant presence means that spring will never arrive (p.136). Like the Memory Police, snow contributes to the disappearance of objects, ensuring that the ground beneath cannot be seen. It first begins to snow after the disappearance of photographs and fruits, and the snow's arrival represents the citizens' emotional detachment as the objects taken from them become more and more personal.
- *Earthquake*: Symbolises a significant, irreversible change. As the ground literally shifts underneath them, the citizens' lives also undergo a terrifying disruption. For the narrator, the earthquake brings with it the death of the old man, which causes an emotional upheaval.
- *Burning of objects*: Signals death. The destruction of objects through burning is a violent act and represents the loss of a part of the citizens' identities. Although some disappeared objects are placed in the river to be carried away, the most significant and personal disappearances are finalised through fire. This is most significant in the burning of the books, as the sheer amount and strength of the fires emphasises the enormity of this loss.
- *Typewriter*: Represents voice and identity in both the main story and the embedded narrative. The woman in the narrator's novel has her voice trapped in a typewriter and when the typewriter is broken, she becomes literally trapped. When novels disappear in the narrator's world, she becomes a typist. The typewriter, for her, comes to represent the loss of her occupation.
- *Hearts*: A physical representation of memories and the soul. The narrator describes her heart as 'hollow … [and] full of holes' (p.82) and R believes that, like memory, 'a heart has no shape, no limits' (p.81). Hearts become a place of conflict, as the narrator gradually loses her memories, and R becomes determined to stop the decay in her heart (p.146).

# CHAPTER-BY-CHAPTER ANALYSIS

## Chapter 1 (pp.3–7)

**Summary:** *The narrator lives on an island where things – objects, words and ideas – disappear; the narrator, like most people on the island, does not remember things that have been disappeared, but her mother does; the narrator's mother keeps some of these disappeared items in a set of secret drawers and feels a sense of sadness that only she can remember them.*

The opening chapter introduces the key difference between this fictional world and ours: on the narrator's island, objects can disappear so thoroughly that 'no one can even recall what it was that disappeared' (p.4). Ogawa creates a sense of unease as she describes the ordinary types of objects that have vanished, such as ribbons, bells, stamps and perfume. Even in these initial pages, the reader is left to wonder what might disappear next and when something more important might be taken away. The narrator experiences 'an uncertain feeling' (p.5) when she looks at any of the disappeared objects, unable to really focus on them and not even able to smell the perfume her mother has kept (p.6). This sense of loss, not just for the objects themselves but for the memory of them, permeates the novel.

The narrator's mother is a sculptor and can remember all the things that have been disappeared. She keeps many of these disappeared objects hidden in a 'secret place' (p.4) as a way of mourning the loss of things that she treasured. The narrator's mother shares this place with her daughter in the hopes that the narrator will be able to remember the objects if she concentrates. While the narrator feels no sorrow or pain for the disappearance of the things on the island, the reader empathises with the narrator's mother. Like her, we have experienced and remembered the smell of perfume and the feel of a piece of ribbon, and so we are positioned to grieve their loss alongside her.

This chapter also introduces the idea that physical objects that have been disappeared must be collected 'to burn, or bury, or toss into the river' (p.4), mirroring the funeral or burial rites from a variety of cultures.

**Q** How else does Ogawa connect the disappearance of objects with death, or language we might use to describe death, in these opening pages?

## Chapter 2 (pp.8–14)

**Summary:** *The narrator reveals that both her parents have died and she lives alone; her father was an ornithologist – someone who studies birds – and he died before the birds were disappeared; the Memory Police pay a visit to the narrator's house to ransack her father's office and destroy anything related to birds.*

With the introduction of the Memory Police the novel shifts in tone, becoming truly dystopian. The narrator's fear of them, and her inability to even raise her voice against them, emphasises their power and authority, particularly as the Memory Police invade the private space of the home. Ogawa refers to the Memory Police in this chapter almost exclusively in the plural, highlighting their cohesiveness and, by removing their individualism, dehumanising them. This is reinforced by references to their machine-like 'efficient manner' (p.13) and their resistance to the heat (p.14).

The narrator had a close relationship with her father, Ogawa suggests; the narrator expresses her love of frequently visiting him at work. Here he would teach her about the birds he studied, and would lovingly 'support the weight' of the binoculars while they watched the creatures 'take flight' (pp.8–9). The loss of 'the only things' (p.13) the narrator has from her father incites grief and loneliness, as she experiences 'an emptiness that would not be filled' (p.14).

**Q** Why is the disappearance of the birds more significant than the disappearances described in the first chapter?

## Chapter 3 (pp.15–19)

**Summary:** *The narrator is a writer whose novels are about loss and disappearances; each evening she goes for a walk and stops to talk to the old man who used to be a mechanic on the ferry; they are friends, and the narrator gives the first copy of each of her books to the old man.*

The narrator's career as a writer reflects the importance of storytelling in the novel. Her novels each tell 'the story of something that had been disappeared' (p.15), as if even in her writing she cannot escape the reality of her world. Ogawa hints at a sense of pointlessness in the narrator's occupation as the library has books that will 'be tossed out without being cared for' and the bookstores are 'nearly deserted' (p.15). Yet the narrator seems unaffected by this.

The friendship between the narrator and the old man is characterised by simplicity. The old man takes on the role of protector, treating the narrator as though she 'were still a little girl' (p.18). They share memories of the past, but Ogawa instils a sense of dread in her readers as the narrator contemplates the way their memories are 'diminishing day by day' (p.18) and, like the peach they eat together, will soon have completely dissolved.

***Q*** Why does the old man not read the narrator's novels? What does this reveal about him as a character and about the society they live in?

## Chapter 4 (pp.20–6)

**Summary:** *The narrator visits her editor, R, to deliver her manuscript; she witnesses the Memory Police round up a group of people living in a safe house; the narrator and R wonder how the Memory Police know who is still able to remember.*

The 'encounter with the Memory Police' (p.20) emphasises the power the Memory Police hold and the fear they inspire in the residents of the island. People watch 'tensely' and the narrator attempts to hide 'behind a lamp pole' (p.20). All are afraid of 'giving the police reason to notice them' (p.22). There is no attempt to resist when the group of people is taken by the Memory Police, either from the apprehended individuals themselves or those watching, and it is clear that Ogawa is commenting on the societal tendency to ignore acts of injustice in favour of self-preservation.

R, the narrator's editor, is characterised as intelligent and thoughtful. He is aware of the danger of the Memory Police, stating that they are 'lurking everywhere' (p.25) and implying that nowhere is safe from them.

Ogawa suggests that the narrator's career as a writer is a literal act of resistance, as she can 'create something totally new … on an island where everything else is disappearing' (p.25). And yet, the sense of foreboding and dread is revealed once again as the narrator worries about what will happen when the words themselves disappear (p.26), highlighting the connection between language and thought, and between storytelling and identity.

***Q*** Ogawa describes the Memory Police as 'men'. How are gender stereotypes upheld through this characterisation, and what might this reveal about the role of police in this society?

## Chapter 5 (pp.27–39)

**Summary:** *The narrator and the old man prepare for winter; the narrator gives the old man a jumper she has knitted; the Inui family knock on the narrator's basement door in the middle of the night to leave some of her mother's sculptures with her; the Inuis are going to live in a safe house after Professor Inui has been summoned by the Memory Police.*

In this chapter, for the first time, the narrator is required to take action to protect those she cares about. Although the protection she offers the Inui family is small – shelter and some warm milk – it is significant as it reveals her compassion for others and desire to help even though she fears the Memory Police. She questions the necessity of the safe house, asking them to consider whether it is worth giving up their 'whole life' (p.34). Professor Inui implies that the police will murder him as they would do 'anything they felt was necessary to ensure secrecy' (p.34).

This gap in understanding reveals the naivety of the narrator, who cannot yet comprehend the totality of the control that the Memory Police wield over the island and its inhabitants. The Inuis also gift the narrator 'five small sculptures' (p.36), and this passing down of heirloom-like objects foreshadows their death.

### Key point

The narrator takes great care to cut the fingernails of the young boy from the Inui family. Ogawa describes the youthful hands, as well as the interaction between the two characters, with great delicacy. This simple, compassionate act works in stark contrast to the harsh totalitarian regime of the Memory Police, emphasising the humanity of those who are victimised by oppressive forces.

***Q*** How would you describe the relationship between the narrator and the old man?

## Chapter 6 (pp.40–9)

**Summary:** *In the narrator's novel, the woman goes to meet her lover, and compares the church bell tower where she meets him to a lighthouse she remembers from her youth; the narrator processes the disappearance of the Inui family; roses disappear from the island.*

The change in font at the beginning of the chapter signposts that this is the narrator's novel we are reading. The woman in the novel appears fearful even as she goes to meet her lover, and there is a sense of foreboding, emphasised by her recollection of the lighthouse and of the feeling that something is following her.

The narrator has heard nothing from the Inui family, and although she stops by their apartment and the hospital where Professor Inui worked, 'the entire Inui family had simply vanished, as though they had melted into thin air' (p.44). The narrator is particularly struck by the fact that 'no one wondered where the professor had gone or lamented his absence' (p.44). In the same way as the objects disappear on the island, so too do the Inui family. In this instance, though, the narrator attempts to remember them, contemplating what they are doing, and how they are feeling.

The disappearance of the roses is 'the most beautiful disappearance ever' (p.48), suggesting that the characters have some ability to find a positive perspective. However, Ogawa underscores the loss of meaning in this disappearance with something more sinister, as soon thereafter the narrator is 'already unable to remember what this thing called a rose had looked like' (p.49).

***Q*** How does Ogawa use symbolism in this chapter to reveal themes and values?

## Chapter 7 (pp.50–4)

**Summary:** *The narrator and the old man discuss what will happen to the island if things continue to disappear; the old man tells the narrator not to worry about this.*

Two contrasting perspectives are offered in this chapter, as both the old man and the narrator come to terms with the loss of the roses. While the narrator worries that the 'island will soon be nothing but absences and holes' (p.53) and that humans themselves will disappear, the old man encourages her to ignore this possible threat, saying that he's 'never really been frightened or particularly missed' (p.53) anything that was disappeared. The old man also echoes the self-preservationist approach of other characters in the novel, saying that 'those Memory Police are only after people who aren't able to forget' (p.54), without seeming to have any particular sympathy for these people.

### Key point

The conversation between the narrator and the old man could be interpreted as reflecting a broader generation gap. Traditionally, younger people are considered more likely to be concerned about social issues than older people. Older people might also be more likely to trust authorities.

***Q*** Why is the old man's perspective in this chapter problematic?

## Chapter 8 (pp.55–63)

**Summary:** *In the narrator's novel, the woman has lost her voice and must use a typewriter to communicate; she asks her lover, the typing teacher, for an ink ribbon for her birthday; R visits the narrator to work on her novel; R requests to look at the narrator's basement, where her mother worked; R reveals that he hasn't forgotten what's been disappeared.*

In the narrator's novel, the woman's loss of voice signals a loss of identity. The power dynamic in the relationship between the woman and the typing teacher becomes clear, as the typing teacher provides her with the ink ribbons that are her voice. Similarly to the previous time we met her, the woman seems to live in a continual state of fear, making the reader distrust her lover and the situation it seems he has placed her in.

In the narrator's world, Ogawa emphasises that work is central to the narrator's relationship with R, as she 'knew nothing else about him' (p.58) except that he reads her manuscripts. Like her mother, when shown the cabinet of secret drawers, R tries to get the narrator to remember the objects. This connection portrays him sympathetically, but also makes us worry for him as we know what the consequences were for the narrator's mother. R's revelation at the end of the chapter, that he hasn't 'forgotten anything' (p.63), reveals the trust he has for the narrator – it has been made very clear how dangerous this knowledge is, for both R and the narrator.

***Q*** Why is it unusual that the narrator's mother only needed three things to get her sculpting done?

## Chapter 9 (pp.64–71)

**Summary:** *The narrator decides to build somewhere R can hide; she asks the old man to help her and he agrees; they plan carefully and prepare a secret space in the narrator's house for R to live in hiding.*

Despite the old man's previous self-preservationist attitude, he agrees to help the narrator before he even knows what she is asking of him.

Ogawa makes clear the thoughtfulness and consideration the narrator and the old man have for R, not just for his necessities, but for things that will help him to retain communication with the outside world (pp.70–1). Having emphasised the brutality and ruthlessness of the Memory Police, Ogawa encourages us to see the act of bravery the narrator and the old man are performing, and the danger and risks they face in helping R. Even the act of entering the hidden room is challenging (p.71).

## Chapter 10 (pp.72–8)

**Summary:** *The narrator tells R they have a place to hide him; R does not want to leave behind his pregnant wife; R and the old man carry out the plan to get R to the hidden room without anyone noticing.*

The narrator does not ask R if he would like to be hidden, but rather tells him he has to go with her. The sacrifice required by R to go into hiding is made apparent when it is revealed his wife is pregnant with a baby that 'will be born in a month' (p.72). In spite of this, the narrator's fear for R's safety motivates her to convince him, and she frames this decision as a duty, 'a job [he must do] to survive' (p.73). With the plan carried off safely, the genius of the hidden room is presented to R, who calls it a 'cave floating in the sky' (p.77), evoking a sense of magic and fairytales. This whimsy is quickly overtaken by the reality of what R's existence will be, and when the narrator hears his voice 'as though from the depths of a swamp' (p.78) it elicits thoughts of burial and death. And, in a sense, R has died: removed from the world without any real possibility of re-entering it.

## Chapter 11 (pp.79–87)

**Summary:** *R and the narrator fall into a routine; they discuss what it feels like to remember everything; the narrator talks to her new editor; the old man makes contact with R's wife under the guise of being a repairman, and collects the first parcel from her via an old wooden box hidden in the town.*

In this chapter, life is reduced to the minutiae as R and the narrator work out a routine and learn to live with one another. There is a sense of horror and the Gothic as R remains trapped 'under the floor' (p.79). Their conversations centre around the connection between memory and humanity, as the narrator once again relates the disappearances to a physical disintegration of her heart (p.82). R contends with this experience, believing that for him 'even if a memory disappears completely, the heart retains something' (p.82). Their discussion suggests that R's ability to remember makes him more human than the other residents of the island.

The old man's collection of the package from R's wife reverses the disappearance of objects we have seen in the novel thus far. The 'carefully folded clothing and … magazines' (p.86) take on new meaning and 'warmth' (p.87) for the narrator, as it becomes important for them to be delivered to R.

***Q*** What is your impression of R's wife, and the place where she is now living?

## Chapter 12 (pp.88–96)

**Summary:** *In the narrator's novel, the woman describes her first time alone with the typing teacher; the teacher maintains a threatening presence as he corrects her mistakes and then holds her finger to the typewriter, trapping her; the narrator finds jobs for R to do to fill his time; photographs and fruit are disappeared; R begs the narrator not to burn her photographs, but she does anyway.*

The typing teacher becomes increasingly threatening, as the woman in the narrator's novel finds herself alone with him and he hovers over her. Ogawa repeatedly describes the woman as feeling 'oppressed' in his presence (p.91) and reiterates her feelings of fear. The description of the woman's anxiety about being 'locked inside the typewriter' (p.92) at the end of this section foreshadows her eventual imprisonment and loss of voice.

The disappearance of the photographs creates conflict between R and the narrator. For the narrator, the loss of the photographs is no tragedy as she has already ceased to remember why they were so precious to her. R, however, understands that the photographs helped her remember her parents and he fears that losing the photos will mean she will lose her parents more completely.

***Q*** Why does R want 'some sort of work to do' (p.93)? What sort of work does the narrator give him and what is the significance of this?

## Chapter 13 (pp.97–112)

**Summary:** *The old man is taken by the Memory Police; R attempts to calm the narrator, who is worried not only for the old man but also that the Memory Police might find R; the narrator visits the headquarters of the Memory Police in the hopes of seeing the old man; she is unsuccessful and is instead interviewed herself by a member of the Memory Police; R and the narrator converse using the funnels of their constructed communication system.*

Although it is R who has the most to lose if they are found out by the Memory Police, it is he who is the voice of reason in this chapter. He remains calm and rational when the narrator expresses fear for both him and the old man, and even offers to leave, proving that he is willing to sacrifice himself in order for the narrator to feel safe. Finally, he offers physical comfort to the narrator, deepening their friendship to something more intimate as he holds her 'in his arms for a long while' (p.99).

The narrator's visit to the headquarters of the Memory Police is an act of bravery that, while highly dangerous, is admirable. Rather than revealing more information about the police and how they operate, the narrator's visit serves only to add further layers to their secrecy: no questions are answered and no suspicions are confirmed. The man who speaks with the narrator is polite and professional, but the lack of threat is in itself threatening, as he is so sure of his control that he does not need to resort to violence of any kind.

***Q*** How does Ogawa reveal the power of the Memory Police in this chapter? What symbols are present that reinforce their status?

## Chapter 14 (pp.113–24)

**Summary:** *The old man returns; he has been interrogated by the Memory Police about a group of people who escaped from the island by boat; the narrator visits the wooden box where R's wife leaves messages and finds out that she has had her baby; the narrator delivers the portrait of R's new son to him.*

The potential escape of some inhabitants of the island is surprising to the narrator and the old man, who had not considered you could 'get away by crossing the sea' (p.114). There are clear parallels to the plight of refugees in our own world who seek asylum by boat, willing to risk drowning at sea or capture to escape their difficult circumstances. The narrator and the old man contemplate how such 'people whose hearts aren't empty' live in hope of finding a place where they 'can go on living' (p.117).

### Key point

The inference that life on the island is akin to death is juxtaposed with the news of the birth of R's son. And, while the narrator treks through the snow – a symbol of disappearance and the silencing of the world – when she retrieves the package from the drop-off point, the snow 'broke into pieces' (p.119). This signifies hope that there are still things that can be created in this place where everything is slowly disappearing.

***Q*** What is the purpose of the story about the servants polishing silver? The text is unclear as to whether this is a historical event, or a story the narrator has made up – what do you think?

## Chapter 15 (pp.125–36)

**Summary:** *In the narrator's novel, the woman's typewriter ceases to work; the typing teacher takes her to the top of the church tower under the impression that he will fix it; instead, he traps her there and tells her he has taken her voice and that she doesn't need it anymore; in the narrator's world, the calendars are disappeared, and the hope of spring along with them.*

The threat that has been hanging over the woman in the narrator's novel is finally realised, whereby she is reduced to an object for the typing teacher to possess. Although she remains tense and fearful, the true horror of her situation seems to be realised only by the reader, as the woman herself can no longer voice her terror. Ogawa makes clear that the ability to give voice to our thoughts and ideas provides us with our identity, which is particularly apparent when the typing teacher informs the woman she has 'lost the ability to make sense of [herself]' (p.132). A pattern of gendered violence is uncovered, as it becomes clear the typing teacher has taken the voices of many young woman who he believes should be 'all silent' (p.131) given they're 'all useless' (p.129).

For the narrator, the loss of the calendars seems easy to process, but as the other residents of her street discuss the diminishing food supply (p.134) and the long winter, she begins to realise that 'with the calendars gone ... spring will never come' (p.135). This trapping in perpetual winter signals the loss of hope, paralleling the imprisonment of the woman in the church tower.

***Q*** How does Ogawa create a sense of foreboding in this chapter?

## Chapter 16 (pp.137–48)

**Summary:** *The narrator carefully shops for ingredients for a meal and for a present in order to celebrate the old man's birthday; the narrator, R and the old man gather in R's hidden room to mark the occasion; R gives the old man an* orugōru *(a music box), an object that has been disappeared.*

The narrator's quest to find ingredients for a birthday meal for the old man reveals the issue of food insecurity, and the daily challenges for all the inhabitants of the island in procuring food. This emphasises the dystopian nature of the island, as the very real threat of starvation increases. In spite of this, the narrator's interactions with the butcher and the fishmonger (p.139) highlight the importance of community and how the citizens are able to show compassion for one another. This is demonstrated too in the narrator's gift of the celery to the old beggar woman (p.138).

The celebration of the old man's birthday, which occurs in the hidden room, and despite the loss of the calendars, is an act of resistance. The characters are willing to risk their lives to mark this milestone. This is highlighted through Ogawa's emphasis on the physical objects at the birthday party: the table setting, the food itself, the dishes and platters, the gifts. All are described in detail, with close attention paid to their materiality which, in the face of the many objects that have been taken from them, becomes a significant reminder of what they still have and how important it is for them to value these things.

***Q*** Why do you think R gives the old man his *orugōru*? What might the *orugōru* symbolise?

## Chapter 17 (pp.149–59)

**Summary:** *The Memory Police search the narrator's house; in spite of their brutal efficiency, they do not find the hidden room; the residents of the street gather outside and watch as three people are taken away by the police; the narrator weeps in the hidden room and R comforts her; they kiss.*

The ease with which the Memory Police are able to enter the narrator's home and ruthlessly search it displays their power and authority. The narrator's fear builds tension and, like the narrator, the reader becomes fixated on the turned-up corner of the rug (p.153). This tiny detail underscores how dangerous their situation is – the three of them could be killed over something so insignificant – and the level of vigilance required to remain safe.

The narrator finds comfort in R's presence, stating that it's 'peaceful to be in such a tiny space' with him (p.156). The friendship they have shared develops in this chapter, in the face of the narrator's overwhelming emotions. The feeling that she is becoming less human – that her 'heart is so weak' (p.158) – is juxtaposed with the very human need for connection and companionship, and so it comes as no surprise that R covers '[her] lips with his' (p.159).

***Q*** How does the narrator feel about the boy who was taken away? How has her perspective changed since the beginning of the novel?

## Chapter 18 (pp.160–70)

**Summary:** *In the narrator's novel, the woman describes her entrapment in the tower; the fearful control of the typing teacher becomes more physical as he progresses to sexual assault; the narrator worries about R avoiding her after they slept together; she listens to R washing himself via their communication tube and imagines each action he is taking.*

The woman in the narrator's novel closely parallels the narrator's own experiences, as they both become more trapped, and suffer more deeply from the control of a menacing outside presence. This can be seen through the woman reinforcing that the loss of her voice 'is much the same as having one's body go to pieces' (p.165) and through her sudden inability to comprehend the words of the other typing students. In this way, such a deterioration can be seen to reflect the narrator's sense of her own diminishing humanity.

The typing teacher's objectification of the woman is disconcerting in its cruelty, as he finds new ways to dehumanise her (pp.164–5), echoing common patterns of abuse in relationships characterised by domestic violence.

***Q*** How has the narrator's relationship with R changed? Why does she feel a loss of intimacy with him?

## Chapter 19 (pp.171–87)

**Summary:** *The narrator is asked by a woman in the street if she knows anyone who can hide her; the narrator, worried about R and a possible trap by the Memory Police, says she cannot help; the narrator starts looking after her neighbours' dog, since they have been taken by the Memory Police; novels disappear and the residents of the island burn all their books; the narrator hides some with R and decides to keep writing in secret.*

While the situation on the island becomes more dire, the narrator continues to act with compassion, looking after her neighbours' dog, Don, partly out of guilt that there were so many people she was unable to look after. The disappearance of the novels heralds a significant change: it is not only a loss of occupation for the narrator, but a loss of her identity as well. The books become objects without meaning or significance for her, despite her desperate attempts to retain her memory of them.

### Key point

Ogawa makes clear connections in this chapter to the book burnings that occurred in Nazi Germany in 1933, which entailed public mass burnings of literary and political works that were not considered to align with Nazi ideologies, such as those by Jewish or socialist authors. Ogawa even references Heinrich Heine, one such influential German writer whose books were burned during this event, with his quote, 'Men who start by burning books end by burning other men' (p.184). The foreshadowing in this reference reveals the humanity that is lost by burning books.

Unlike the disappearance of other objects, in this instance the narrator and the old man travel all over the island to burn the narrator's novels. The journey required to destroy this part of the narrator's identity highlights the significance of this destruction.

***Q*** Why is the narrator able to remember certain objects in this chapter that have previously been disappeared?

## Chapter 20 (pp.188–97)

**Summary:** *The narrator gets a job as a typist; her new job makes her much busier and she is out of the house all day; she continues to try to write her novel in secret, but is unable to; R encourages her to take her time with it; the old man and the narrator make pancakes and listen to the music box; the old man asks the narrator if she is in love with R; she admits that she is, but that it doesn't matter as he is unable to leave the hidden room; an earthquake occurs.*

The narrator's new job as a typist mirrors that of the woman in the novel that she has been writing, and although the narrator cannot initially remember this, the reader feels a growing sense of horror that the narrator will become as trapped as the woman she wrote about. This is emphasised through the narrator's descriptions of her loss of self: she feels as though she has been 'sucked into the flames' (p.192) and that exhaustion is 'overtaking [her] soul' (p.194). Even the eating of the pancakes themselves, a small moment of joy in their increasingly dystopian world, foreshadows the disappearances to come; as 'the remaining pieces of pancake grew smaller, so [too] did the size of the bites [they] cut' (p.193).

***Q*** What do you think Ogawa is telling us about the importance of art and music in this chapter?

## Chapter 21 (pp.198–205)

**Summary:** *The old man is pinned down by a cabinet that fell during the earthquake, but the narrator rescues him; they escape to high ground to avoid the tsunami, and then return to the narrator's house to assess the damage; the earthquake has warped the floorboards and R is trapped in the hidden room; the old man and the narrator use borrowed tools to free him.*

In this chapter, it is the old man's memories of tsunamis that save them from drowning, suggesting that the experience and memories we share as a community are crucial to our survival. In this novel, where very few people can remember, the community will not be able to survive.

The physical danger of the earthquake does not seem to distress the inhabitants of the island much more than the usual disappearances. This disturbing complacency of the citizens can be seen as part of a larger pattern that facilitates their ignorance and their unwillingness to resist the Memory Police.

***Q*** Why does the old man save the *orugōru*?

## Chapter 22 (pp.206–19)

**Summary:** *The old man goes to live with the narrator; he fixes up the damage from the earthquake; the narrator and the old man find disappeared objects that the narrator's mother had hidden inside her sculptures; the narrator shows them to R, who tells her the story of each of them: the ferry ticket, the harmonica and* ramune.

The discovery of the forgotten objects reinforces the vast quantity of things that have been lost. While these new objects are described as 'dozing' and peaceful (p.218), the old man is not even able to touch them (p.210), suggesting that there is no recuperating what has been lost for him.

The objects share 'a certain gentle modesty' (p.210) and both the narrator and R treat them with care, highlighting again the significance of all objects, not just things that readers might consider important. This is accentuated by the stories that both the narrator and R tell about the objects. The objects are connected to memories that form part of their identity, including their relationships with others.

***Q*** Why do you think the narrator's mother went to such effort to protect these objects?

***Q*** What does each object symbolise?

## Chapter 23 (pp.220–7)

**Summary:** *The narrator and the old man go to the cabin owned by the narrator's mother and collect all the sculptures that are hiding objects that have been disappeared; at the train station on their way home, they are stopped by the Memory Police, who are checking people's papers and luggage; they manage to get to the back of the queue and escape notice; when they arrive home, the old man is unable to use the fork to eat his dinner.*

The dystopian elements of the setting are escalated by the appearance of the Memory Police at the train station. The checking of documentation suggests that the residents of the island are not allowed to leave and are trapped under the control of the authoritarian government. Although there is a sense that this is a routine inspection and hence nothing to fear, still the people in the queue hold their breath (p.225) when a man dares to speak against the imposition of the inspection. Ogawa builds tension in this scene, as the narrator and the old man worry that the Memory Police will check their luggage and find the hidden objects. This tension highlights the culture of fear that exists on the island, and how even everyday actions like taking a train can be upended through the control of the police.

***Q*** How is the old man's inability to use his fork successfully similar to other impairments in the novel?

## Chapter 24 (pp.228–39)

**Summary:** *The narrator and the old man break open the sculptures and share the hidden objects with R; the narrator's adopted dog, Don, has an ear infection and she takes him to the vet; the old man gives R a haircut; the narrator and the old man meet on the hill and have a final conversation.*

The death of the old man in the subsequent chapter brings new meaning to the conversation he has with the narrator on the hill. Ogawa suggests that he is happy and feels lucky to be living with the narrator (p.235), but his acceptance of the tragedies that have befallen him remains disconcerting. In fact, his assertion that he would not 'want to go back to the way it was before' (p.235) seems untrue, even coming from the resilient old man. For once, it is the narrator who assures the old man that he does not have to worry, and that they will 'be able to cope with whatever comes next' (p.238). As the old man dies soon after this, Ogawa seems to imply that they will not, in fact, be able to adapt to the next changes. The narrator's final gift to the old man is the three *ramune* candies: a symbol of the experiences he has lost, and the love and care the narrator has for her friend.

***Q*** What does R's haircut reveal about both R and the old man?

## Chapter 25 (pp.240–51)

**Summary:** *The narrator grieves the death of the old man; it is revealed that he sustained a head trauma during the earthquake, which eventually killed him; the narrator begins to write again; the next things to disappear are left legs; the inhabitants of the island struggle more than usual with this new obstacle, but eventually accept this disappearance as they have the others.*

For the first time, a disappearance causes a physical alteration, rather than an emotional or mental shift. The loss of her left leg creates problems for the narrator as she dresses and attempts to navigate the stairs in her house. Even her neighbour the hatmaker reports feeling as though his body has 'gone to pieces and won't go back together again' (p.248), revealing an understated violence to this disappearance. The ability of the Memory Police to walk 'perfectly in balance' (p.249) causes us to question whether the Memory Police have retained their memories, allowing them to maintain even more power over the inhabitants of the island. R and the narrator remain close, and the way R massages the narrator's disappeared leg (p.249) highlights the intimacy between them. Even though the narrator cannot feel her left leg, the act does not lose its meaning, as she requests that he continue massaging her in order to feel a greater sense of self.

**Q** Why are the inhabitants of the island so easily able to accept this new trauma?

## Chapter 26 (pp.252–9)

**Summary:** *The number of people taken by the Memory Police increases, as they are unable to hide that they remember their left legs; the narrator sets up a new system of communication with R's wife that is reduced to a number of telephone rings; people's right arms disappear; the narrator keeps writing, and finds the story of her novel slowly coming back to her; she worries about which of her body parts will disappear next, and R tells her it doesn't matter as she can stay in the hidden room with him.*

As the narrator feels herself disappearing, R comforts her. They are both trapped with 'no escape' (p.257), but while R continues to feel strongly connected to the narrator, who he 'can touch any part of' that he wants (p.257), the narrator experiences increasing isolation, as if their hearts are 'being pulled apart to such different, distant places' (p.258). R's words of encouragement seem possessive and falsely optimistic, as there would be no way for them to get food if they both remained in the secret room. There is an intimacy in this desire to be hidden away from the world, but there is also a self-destructive nature to it that is disconcerting.

**Q** How does Ogawa create a sense of dread in this chapter?

## Chapter 27 (pp.260–8)

**Summary:** *The woman in the narrator's novel begins to lose her eyesight; another young girl approaches the door to the tower and knocks, but the woman does not respond; the woman realises, with explanation from the typing teacher, that she is being absorbed into the* *room; the typing teacher comes to see her less and less, until, finally, he brings the new young girl to the tower and the woman disappears.*

This is the only section of the narrator's novel that has its own complete chapter, and this underscores the increasing parallels between the narrator and the woman in her novel. This final section of the narrator's novel reveals the pattern of serial abuse carried out by the typing teacher, as he describes grooming his new students and begins to target another student to eventually replace the woman in the tower.

Like the narrator, the woman has lost not only her sense of self, but a sense of her own materiality: her 'legs seemed to be floating in air' (p.266). In spite of this, the woman cannot help her attachment to the typing teacher, feeling gratitude for the small acts of thoughtfulness he performs and believing that 'everything exists only for him' (p.267). This devotion to someone so cruel is unsettling, and signals just how completely the typing teacher has managed to trap his student.

### Key point

The woman in the narrator's novel could be interpreted as exhibiting Stockholm syndrome, whereby hostages form positive emotional connections to their captors. Such a psychological response is considered to be a survival mechanism in reaction to the trauma associated with being held against one's will. While there is little academic evidence for Stockholm syndrome, it remains an oft-used concept in the media and popular culture.

**Q** Why do you think the woman begins to lose her eyesight? What might this symbolise?

**Q** Why do you think the woman remains attached to the typing teacher despite his poor treatment of her?

## Chapter 28 (pp.269–74)

**Summary:** *The narrator gives her finished manuscript to R; the bodies of the island's inhabitants disappear, but life continues on; eventually, all that is left of the narrator is her voice; she asks R to look after the hidden room in the hope that the memory of her will live on; as her voice disappears, R climbs the ladder to the outside world, and rolls the rug over the trapdoor.*

The inevitable end for the inhabitants of the island arrives, as their bodies disappear until all that remains are their voices. They do not resist this disappearance any more than they have the other disappearances, and this resignation is a brutal reminder of the fate that awaits us all if we choose inaction over action.

While Ogawa provides some hope that R will be 'free to return to the outside world' as the Memory Police are no longer bothering to hunt people (p.273), the final lines of the text reveal something more disturbing: the narrator hears 'the faint sound of the rug being rolled out on the floor' (p.274). The rug's purpose is to keep the secret room hidden, but if the island's inhabitants have all disappeared, there is no need to hide the room, especially if R believes it is possible for the narrator to recall her memories. The narrator has been buried alive in the hidden room, forgotten, but not entirely disappeared.

***Q*** What does the narrator's desire to be remembered tell us about the importance of memory?

# CHARACTERS & RELATIONSHIPS

## The narrator

**Key quotes**

'People—and I'm no exception—seem capable of forgetting almost anything ...' (p.10)

'The new cavities in my heart search for things to burn. They drive me to burn things and I can stop only when everything is in ashes.' (p.95)

'I'd like to leave behind some trace of my existence on the island.' (p.270)

The narrator is a compassionate and resilient character, who adapts to her changing world, even though she feels there is 'no way to fill in the voids left by the Memory Police' (p.16). Initially, she seems to accept the oppressive regime she lives in, but she gradually begins to question the disappearances, and the cruel actions of the Memory Police.

The appearance of the Inuis on her doorstep as they are heading to a hiding place is the catalyst for her to take action, and she decides she'd 'like to try to help someone' (p.66). The narrator then begins to demonstrate acts of bravery, risking her life to hide R and, later, saving the old man from the rubble after an earthquake. Even when a complete stranger approaches her on the street to ask if there is somewhere she can hide, the narrator's first instinct is to help her. This empathy continues to guide her actions, as she also takes in an abandoned dog, giving him

> all the love and care [she] wished [she] could give to the couple who had been his owners, the boy who had been hidden in their house, the Inui family, and Mizore, their cat. (p.175)

## Key point

Although the narrator's job is one of creation 'on an island where everything else is disappearing' (p.25), she still feels the impact of the disappearances, and feels she has 'no strength to resist' (p.95). The physical toll of the disappearances seems to weaken her, but she does make some effort to resist, continuing to write her novel even after novels are disappeared. This resilience and determination contribute to our understanding of her courage, as we can see how much easier it would be for her to accept the loss, particularly with the threat of the Memory Police looming so close.

The narrator's friendship with R shapes her, as he is 'the friend who knows the self that [she puts] in [her] novels better than anyone else' (p.66). They become more intimate throughout the novel and take 'refuge' (p.168) in one another, sharing a private space where they can escape the oppressive control of the Memory Police, if only for a little while. It is R's encouragement that motivates her to continue writing, emphasising the significance of this relationship.

However, the narrator begins to realise that she and R are growing apart and, 'try as [they] might to understand each other' (p.176), they cannot reconcile their differences. 'An important bond between the two of [them] is ... cut' (p.176) as the narrator loses more and more of her memories, and she feels she has become materially different from R, who retains his ability to remember. This is exemplified in the simile where the narrator describes trying to connect with R 'as though [she] were trying to glue a pebble [she'd] found in the garden to an origami figure' (p.242). She fears losing her body entirely, 'not because [she'll] disappear and cease to exist' (p.259), but because it will mean leaving R. When the end does come, she returns to the acceptance with which she approached her life at the beginning of the text, stating that it is 'peaceful with just a voice' (p.273), although it is clear that this end is horrifying, and could be considered a violation of her very body.

## The Memory Police

### Key quotes

'Our primary function here is to assure that there are no delays in the process and that useless memories disappear quickly and easily.' (p.106)

'Their operation proceeded as it always did. Efficiently, thoroughly, systemically, and without any trace of emotion.' (p.150)

The Memory Police is the powerful and authoritarian group whose 'first duty' is to 'enforce the disappearances' (p.14). It is a mysterious and secretive institution, which first appeared after the disappearances began. Its members carry out inspections 'with terrible efficiency' (p.21) and are often described as inhuman, with emphasis placed on their lack of emotion and the robotic way they carry out their tasks.

Their methods for finding objects that have been disappeared, and for finding people who retain all their memories, become 'more and more brutal' (p.64) as the disappearances increase. The Memory Police maintain an aura of fear, underscored by all the symbols of their power: their badges and tassels, their green covered trucks, and 'their long, carefully tailored coats' that make them seem 'as though they were looking down menacingly on everything around them' (p.152).

Like the government and military bodies in the real world that they are allegories for, the Memory Police seem to be above the laws they enforce. The disappearances themselves appear to cause the Memory Police 'no difficulty' (p.249) and they receive luxuries the other inhabitants of the island are not afforded, such as a stable supply of food (p.225). It is significant, too, that no female officers of the Memory Police are mentioned. This cruel, authoritarian force that invades homes and takes people away to secret locations is comprised entirely of men, inferring both that there is something innately threatening about masculinity, and also that it is often men who are responsible for such brutal acts, fictional or not.

**Key point**

The Memory Police is portrayed as a terrifying, relentless force; however, by the end of the text its officers are no longer actively hunting people down. The world 'is in ruins, crushed under the weight of the snow' (p.273) and the control of the Memory Police. They have been so successful in establishing a pervasive and all-encompassing system of power that they no longer need to pursue individuals who may be resisting.

## R

**Key quotes**

'But I remember ... The beauty of the emerald and the smell of perfume. I haven't forgotten anything.' (p.63)

'No matter what disappeared next, no matter how close the Memory Police came to finding us, he could do nothing but remain in the secret room.' (p.228)

As the only significant character who retains their memories of the disappeared objects, R often echoes the thoughts and emotions of the reader. He is thoughtful and intelligent, mentoring the narrator in his job as her editor, and intent on restoring her memories in his role as her friend. R sacrifices his way of life, and agrees to hide in the narrator's secret room, as a 'way to save not just [himself], but [his] wife and baby too' (p.73). This self-sacrificial attitude is evident later when he is nearly discovered by the Memory Police and he offers to leave if the narrator wants him to, in order to protect her (p.99).

Initially kind and reserved, R becomes less placid as the disappearances increase, desperate to 'help delay or stop this decay' (p.146) in the hearts of the narrator and the old man. He is 'violently opposed' (p.175) to the burning of the books, and remains optimistic that the memories might be restored if only the narrator and the old man try harder to remember.

R's existence in the hidden room is suffocating, and the narrator wonders if his body has 'actually begun to shrink since he'd hidden himself away' (p.119). Yet, even as his life is reduced to trivial daily tasks, with no connection to the outside world, his soul remains full and 'dense' (p.196), unlike those around him. His relationship with the narrator becomes more intimate, as they seek physical comfort from one another. This betrayal of his wife is understandable, given that it seems unlikely he will ever see her again, and given how small and meaningless his life has become. The narrator describes it as her job to 'go on holding him here at the bottom of the sea' (p.196), although it is almost always R who takes the narrator 'in his arms' (p.99).

### Key point

R is the only character for whom we have any hope at the end of the novel, as he leaves the hidden room and rejoins the outside world, with sunlight – symbolic of freedom – 'streaming in for one moment' (p.274). He seems reluctant to leave the narrator behind, especially as he had taken such care of her as her body slowly disappeared. And yet, he rolls the rug over the trapdoor, effectively burying the narrator, leaving us to question his real motivations.

## The old man

### Key quotes

'He was truly gifted when it comes to machines, food, and plants.' (p.17)

'You have to stop worrying about things like that. The disappearances are beyond our control. They have nothing to do with us. We're all going to die anyway, someday, so what's the difference? We simply have to leave things to fate.' (p.185)

The old man acts as a father figure to the narrator, supporting and encouraging her in a variety of ways. He has a nurturing disposition, and seeks to look after the narrator, and then R, through acts of service: equipping the secret room, being the go-between for R and his wife, cooking for the narrator. When he is given something, the old man holds out 'both hands to receive it, as he might have when making an offering at the household altar' (p.143), exhibiting a depth of gratitude close to worship.

Unlike R and the narrator, the old man is entirely accepting of the disappearances, displaying a detachment verging on naivety. He claims not to have been 'frightened' nor to have 'particularly missed' any of the disappeared objects 'when they were gone' (p.53), and frequently tells the narrator that 'there's nothing for [her] to worry [herself] over' (p.51). This emotional detachment could be seen as a form of self-preservation, or a way to cope with the constant turmoil of the disappearances.

As his friendship with R develops, the old man shows a willingness to resist the inevitable loss of his memories, wanting to support R even in something he thinks is pointless. He expresses these feelings of helplessness throughout the novel, believing that 'even if [they] resist the Memory Police, [they] can't resist the fate that separates [them] from R' (p.237). In spite of this, he cherishes his friends, and clearly values the sense of community they have built together, particularly after the earthquake, when they 'did not need to move, content to hold hands and stare at one another for a long time' (p.205).

## Key point

The old man's death occurs not because of the disappearances, but due to the earthquake, highlighting the fragility and arbitrary nature of life. We are left to question whether it is the disappearances that have caused him such loss – of his occupation, his home, his physical abilities – or if these are simply the consequences of old age.

## The woman

### Key quotes

'I held my breath, unable to move, as though locked inside the typewriter.' (p.92)

'I knew now that I lacked the courage to rejoin the outside world.' (p.262)

The woman in the narrator's novel comes to represent not just the narrator, but all the inhabitants of the island, who find their experience of the world progressively limited. Like the citizens of the narrator's world, the woman feels her existence 'being sucked away to some remote and inaccessible place' (p.266), as she loses first her voice, then her sight, and then her sense of her own body. Her entrapment in a church tower provides a fairytale element to her imprisonment, but hers is a story of misery and despair as she begins to feel her 'body growing more distant from [her] soul' (p.166). The loss of her voice symbolises her loss of agency. She has no control over her circumstances, and cannot even bring herself to escape when opportunity presents itself.

Her relationship with her typing teacher is similarly miserable. Although she describes him as her lover, the fear that characterises their relationship is present from the beginning as she climbs slowly to meet him 'listening carefully to each step' (p.42). She is 'increasingly oppressed, as though [she] were being backed into a corner by a powerful force' (p.91). And yet, in spite of this, she is completely reliant on him, believing he is the 'only thing holding [her] together' (p.167).

### Key point

The woman is a victim of the typing teacher's abuse, and her fate seems as inevitable as that of the narrator. She is 'absorbed' (p.264) into the tower room, completely destroyed by the teacher's abuse. We are left with a deep sense of horror, emphasised by this ending's juxtaposition with the surreal and almost childlike elements of the story, such as the voices trapped in typewriters.

## The typing teacher

### Key quotes

'You have no need to talk, no need to utter a single word. There's nothing to worry about, nothing to fear. Then, at last, you'll be all mine.' (p.131)

'I was glad that I was able to erase your voice.' (p.132)

The detached abuse of the typing teacher in the narrator's novel is horrifying, but also recognisable. His grooming of young women mirrors similar behaviour we might see or witness being reported in the real world, and it is clear he uses his authority as a teacher to maintain control over all of his students, training them to accept his punishments and normalising his threatening presence.

He pays attention to the woman in the narrator's novel, but 'treats [her] just as he pleases' (p.163), and as such his care seems sinister and controlling, rather than loving. His cruelty is enacted upon the woman's body: he smiles 'with satisfaction' as she forces herself into 'strangely shaped garments' (p.165), he washes her, and he selects the food she eats and watches her eat it mouthful by mouthful.

His cycle of abuse is completed when he brings a new young woman to the tower, and the narrator's protagonist is absorbed into the room. The pile of typewriters in the corner suggests the sheer number of women he has violated in this way, erasing their voices and then their bodies.

### Key point

The portrayal of the typing teacher initially suggests parallels to the oppressive nature of the Memory Police, emphasising emotional and physical control over others. However, there are unsettling connections between the typing teacher and R, who both seem to want to control the identity of the woman they care for. While R's intentions may not be malevolent, there is a hint of possessiveness in his actions. The narrator's perspective, as the one writing the novel, introduces a layer of uncertainty about her true feelings towards R and the extent of her agency in their relationship. As the narrator gradually loses autonomy, it is R who must care for her, and we might question whether she feels R is partly to blame for her loss of identity, as the typing teacher is to blame in the novel.

# THEMES, IDEAS & VALUES

## Disappearance and loss

### Key quotes

'The island is run by men who are determined to see things disappear ... they force it to disappear with their own hands.' (p.25)

'... every last bit of me will disappear.' (p.257)

The disappearance of things is the central conflict of *The Memory Police*. As the inhabitants of the island lose hats, birds, roses and calendars, it is not just the objects themselves that vanish, but also the ability of the citizens to recall them at all. The absence of these objects disrupts the inhabitants' daily lives, eroding their sense of familiarity and stability. The disappearances seem 'to be speeding up' (p.53) and the old man remembers that when he was a child the island seemed 'a lot fuller, a lot more real' (p.54), suggesting that the disappearances contribute to a loss of reality. For those who remember, it is impossible to 'imagine what these disappearances mean' (p.24) and how it alters the perspective and experiences of those around them.

It is not merely objects that are disappeared, but people. Those who retain their memories of things are hunted by the Memory Police and taken to undisclosed locations. The narrator's mother and Professor Inui are sent for by the police, and although the narrator is told that her mother died of a heart attack (p.33), Ogawa implies that she was killed because she could remember the disappeared things. The atmosphere of fear created by these abductions means that even those who do not remember lose their sense of safety. The disappearances of people mirror real-world government actions, both historical and contemporary. Ogawa seems to be criticising governments and political groups who arrest people who have committed no criminal acts, but instead possess a trait they have no control over.

The island itself almost disappears as well, 'crushed under the weight of the snow' (p.273). The old man's boat 'sank completely beneath the surface of the sea' (p.271) and the atmosphere of the island is 'full of holes' (p.270). It is a clear allegory for climate change, and what will happen to Earth if no action is taken. Like on the island, real-world disappearances of plant and animal species seem to cause no great alarm, and the ozone layer literally, rather than figuratively, has holes.

## Memory

### Key quotes

'... I don't even know what it is I should be remembering. What's gone is gone completely. I have no seeds inside me, waiting to sprout again.' (p.82)

'We're all free to do as we choose with our own memories ...' (p.231)

The loss of the memory of the disappeared objects is the most noticeable change the island inhabitants experience. Memories shape identity and losing them results in an erasure of the past and an erosion of both society and individual selfhood. The disappearance of the birds causes not just the loss of the creatures themselves, but of all references to them. The narrator, whose father was an ornithologist, watches as the Memory Police destroy a photograph of her family simply because it contained a 'brightly colored rare bird' (p.14).

When the photographs themselves are disappeared, the narrator struggles to grapple with this loss, as 'they brought back wonderful memories ... memories that made [her] heart ache' (p.94). For the narrator, whose parents have both died, this disappearance diminishes the connection she had with them, as now the photographs are 'nothing more than pieces of paper' (p.95).

However, it is not just the narrator who suffers in this way, and as more and more things vanish, the inhabitants of the island gradually lose their collective history, cultural heritage and shared narratives. This collective amnesia perpetuates a sense of disorientation and detachment from the past, resulting in a society disconnected from itself.

**Key point**

Ogawa positions us to see the importance and necessity of memories, not just for individuals for whom these memories provide points of reference and connection, but for society, as memories help us understand our history. The danger of losing these memories, she suggests, is that we will lose everything: our identities, our relationships and our humanity.

## Grief

**Key quotes**

'But I'm not sure the word "crying" did justice to what I was experiencing. Clearly, it was not a matter of being sad. Nor was it just relief from the tension I had felt.' (p.157)

'I found it terribly difficult to come to terms with the old man's death.' (p.242)

The losses experienced by the narrator eventually extend to the people she is close to, and the death of the old man profoundly moves her. She feels as though his death 'had suddenly transformed the very ground under [her] feet into a soft, unreliable mass' (p.242). Amidst her detached acceptance of the other disappearances, it is jarring to observe the narrator's deep grief at the loss of her friend. We might question whether her heart really is hollow or whether, in order to survive in this society, it is necessary to distance yourself from loss. The narrator experiences a loss of purpose, feeling that 'nothing was likely to interest [her] soul in its weakened state' (p.243).

We are not given insight into the grief that R, separated from his wife and child, must be feeling. However, the implication in the narrator's mother's sadness when asked 'Why are you the only one who hasn't lost anything? Do you remember everything? Forever?' (p.7) is that those who can remember experience a much deeper sense of grief. These individuals watch on as their friends and family change beyond recognition, and there is no one with whom they can share their memories.

## Identity and agency

### Key quotes

'When you lost your voice, you lost the ability to make sense of yourself.' (p.132)

'Your soul is trying to bring back the things it lost in the disappearances.' (p.245)

The disappearances mean that many characters lose their occupations or jobs, and it is clear through the narrator's use of their occupations to name them (the hatmaker, the fishmonger, the butcher) that these roles are closely tied to their identity. This is evidenced in the characterisation of the narrator's ornithologist father for whom 'identifying those wild creatures was his one true gift' (p.9). When the novels disappear, the narrator herself must find a new profession, and she struggles with the loss of self that this change enforces. The idea that writing is a type of art, and that art is a creative and soulful practice, is upheld in the novel, suggesting that the narrator can no longer fully express herself.

The narrator exhibits agency through her decision to hide R. She resists the passive attitudes of her neighbours and decides that it is more important to act with compassion. She is not the only one who makes this decision, however, as it is clear that there are many people being hidden from the Memory Police. And while this act of resistance empowers individuals to exert some control over their lives and the lives of others, their lack of agency in this society is more obvious when they come physically into contact with the Memory Police. It is the Memory Police who give orders and maintain power, requiring their citizens to submit or be taken away.

Identity can also be seen to be inextricably linked to memories. The characters who are able to remember seem fuller and more real than their counterparts who are affected by the disappearances. As the disappearances increase, the inhabitants of the island who forget gradually lose their sense of self, until even their physical bodies disappear. By the end of the novel, the narrator becomes just a mere voice that can drift 'aimlessly' and 'slip through' cracks (p.272). The loss of bodily autonomy represents the ultimate surrender of her agency, rendering her powerless and confined within her own voice. The narrator is physically detached from the world, and therefore has no ability to act or shape her own destiny. Her voiced identity has little meaning without her body, reflecting the pervasive control of the Memory Police, who have been able to subject the inhabitants of the island to such total submission of self.

In the narrator's novel, the woman loses her voice, and is stripped of her ability to communicate effectively. The physical disability means she can no longer express herself and renders her entirely reliant on the typing teacher, eroding her autonomy and making her vulnerable to the whims of others. We are positioned to see the horror of this: not being able to request even our most simple needs and relying on the choices of another person to ensure we survive.

## Isolation

### Key quotes

'You have to hide by yourself.' (p.73)

'... the best way to keep him safe was to keep him completely isolated.' (p.253)

The hidden room in the narrator's house serves as a symbol of physical isolation. While it is a space of safety for R, it is also 'far removed from the outside world' (p.67), to the extent that R cannot even imagine the world beyond the room, feeling as though 'there's nothing on the other side, no connection to anything else' (p.109). Even accessing the hidden room is a physical challenge, meaning that it is, for someone 'as large as R' (p.71), almost impossible to leave. Although R does not complain about his isolation, Ogawa portrays the difficulty of living in such a small space with nothing to occupy your time, and we are positioned to see the suffering that R endures to protect himself and his family.

R is isolated both physically and emotionally from his wife and child. While initially they are able to communicate via letter, eventually this becomes too dangerous, and they must resort to letting 'the phone ring three times at a predetermined hour before hanging up' to signal that 'R was healthy and doing well' (p.253). With the absence of any real communication, R's only connection to the outside world is through the narrator, leaving him almost entirely detached from reality.

The woman in the embedded narrative lives, like R, in a small room. The clock tower is not a place of safety for her, though; it is a prison. Unlike R, the woman can see and hear the outside world, at least initially, but cannot participate in it, and this closeness to freedom highlights just how painful her entrapment is. In much the same way, the island itself is separated from the world. There are no means of transport to other islands or locations anymore, and attempting to leave the island puts you at risk of drowning or being captured by the Memory Police.

The characters in *The Memory Police* are also profoundly affected by emotional isolation. The loss of the narrator's parents ought to cause her immense grief, but she relays their deaths with detachment and emotional numbness: 'My mother died, and then my father died, and since then I have lived all alone in this house' (p.8). This emotional disconnect is also evident in the increasing separation between the narrator and R, despite their physical proximity and closeness. As more objects and memories disappear, the difference in their experience of the world increases and they are unable to truly understand one another. Even when they are physically intimate, the narrator feels distanced from R, particularly as more and more of her body disappears. She yearns to 'feel his lips, to sense them on skin and flesh that had not disappeared' but instead feels 'only a slight pressure, like the weight of a bit of modeling clay' (p.251). We are positioned to empathise with this experience of isolation, and also to see its inevitability given their different situations.

## Importance of community

### Key quotes

'… you can trust me. There's nothing to worry about and I'll take care of everything.' (p.74)

'It had been a long time since any of us had been so jolly.' (p.140)

In the face of such complete isolation, Ogawa highlights the importance of community. The citizens of the island readily assist one another, as the narrator gives 'the celery to an old beggar woman' (p.138), and the shop owners who 'were both friends of the old man' (p.139) supply meat and fish for his birthday despite the food shortages. This particular occasion of the old man's birthday is characterised by the joy of celebrating together. The narrator, R and the old man are 'jolly' and 'more talkative than usual' (p.140), revealing the pleasure that a sense of community can provide.

Each disappearance is marked by a need for connection, as the neighbours gather to destroy what was lost and discuss what it might mean for their lives. This communal processing of loss possibly makes it easier for them to accept the disappearances.

### Key point

Ogawa makes clear the importance of community in ensuring histories and memories are not lost. R believes that 'no matter how wonderful the memory, it vanishes if you leave it alone, if no one pays attention to it' (p.231), revealing the power of people sharing in conversation and discussion.

## Complacency and resistance

### Key quotes

'Don't worry. It's no good overthinking this. Calendars are just scraps of paper. Be patient. It will all work itself out.' (p.136)

'There was no uproar, no confusion. We merely went about our usual morning routines, accepting that a new cavity had opened in our lives.' (p.256)

Despite the losses they suffer each time something new disappears, the citizens of the island are 'quite accustomed to these' (p.65) and accept the upheaval in their life calmly. The narrator asserts that 'no one ever complains' (p.15) and in fact the citizens sometimes approach the disappearances with humour, such as the old woman who claims she's 'actually lucky' that her leg has disappeared as 'half the arthritis in [her] knees is gone' (p.248). The inhabitants of the island are concerned merely with how easily they will be able to continue on with their lives, and refuse to consider the possible consequences of such naive acceptance. Even when their limbs begin to disappear, they learn 'to control [their] bodies without too much inconvenience' (p.252).

Ogawa suggests that the consequence of passive acceptance is death. While the citizens 'were not afraid', they 'made no attempt to escape their fate' (p.269). The old man maintains that 'there's no reason to think [the Memory Police will] go further anytime soon' (p.184) despite the increasing frequency and significance of the disappearances. His characterisation and eventual death is a clear warning for readers who might be tempted to adopt a similar attitude.

The narrator initially shares in this complacency, unable to understand why the Inuis would want to escape when they will be 'giving up [their] work, [their] whole life' (p.34). Like the old man, she is inclined to believe that 'there's nothing too terrible about things disappearing' and that she is in no real danger as 'those Memory Police are only after people who aren't able to forget' (p.54). However, as R reveals his secret, it becomes harder for her to ignore that there are many people in danger, including potentially herself, and she begins to resist the control of the Memory Police.

Although there is a sense that 'no one can escape' the Memory Police (p.25), there exists 'a fairly large underground network that creates … safe houses and then keeps them running' (p.23). This illustrates the large number of people who are unwilling to resign themselves to the changes in their society, and instead risk their own safety to help others. At one point the former hatmaker is shocked at the idea his neighbours were 'hiding people' (p.155), suggesting that they were quite unremarkable. We are led to see that it is not unusually heroic to protect others, but the responsibility of all citizens.

Those who retain their memories seem more inclined to resist the authority of the Memory Police. The narrator's mother hides disappeared objects in her sculptures, and R encourages the narrator and the old man to hold and use these objects. Through these characters, Ogawa emphasises the necessity of resistance. As readers, it is R and the narrator's mother who are most relatable, as we too retain our memories and like them understand the significance and destructive consequences of the disappearances.

### Key point

Small acts of resistance do not appear to make much of an impact, such as the narrator's decision to 'go on writing [her novels] in secret' (p.185) or the old man listening to 'the music box hidden in the bathroom' (p.194). Yet Ogawa encourages us to see that these actions, however minor, allow the characters to retain some of their humanity, and that it is the striving for this that is important.

## Danger and risk

### Key quotes

'They weren't interested in my name and address; they were testing me. So the important thing was to remain calm, to act naturally.' (p.107)

'... if one of the officers were to reach in to search or empty the contents completely, that would be the end of us. There was nowhere to run. My mouth was dry as dust, my tongue glued to the roof.' (p.224)

Resisting the rules of the Memory Police requires individuals to put themselves in danger. However, the novel suggests that this danger is short term, and the greater danger is the casual acceptance of the Memory Police's control, which will eventually result in the disappearance of everything. There are those willing to trust total strangers, such as the woman who approaches the narrator in the street and asks if she knows somewhere to hide (p.171). Although the narrator doubts the authenticity of the request, the fact that she doesn't immediately dismiss it reveals that the Memory Police are a far greater danger than individual citizens. The narrator slowly comes to understand that 'the more deeply' she becomes involved in helping others, 'the more danger [she'll] be in' (p.38) and recognises that hiding R 'could cost' their lives (p.66).

We are positioned to admire the narrator for risking her life for another and, by extension, to admire real-world examples of people who endanger themselves to help others, such as those who hid Jewish families throughout Europe during World War II.

## Storytelling

### Key quotes

'But even if the paper itself disappears, words will remain. It will be all right, you'll see. We haven't lost the stories.' (p.191)

'A mind that we cannot see has created a story that we can. They may have burned the novels, but your heart did not disappear.' (p.231)

As a fictional story, the novel itself is a vehicle for the message that storytelling is crucial to our humanity. Elements of storytelling are frequent throughout the text as the narrator often concludes sections with 'so it was', suggesting that the events unfolding are being narrated. There are examples of foreshadowing, too, that contribute to this, such as the acknowledgement that 'in the end … the old woman's prediction … turned out to be accurate' (p.136).

The narrator's novel adds another layer of storytelling as she reflects on the process of writing. Her struggle to complete her novel speaks to the power and resilience of storytelling, that even when 'words seem to retreat further and further away' it is necessary 'to go on writing' (p.82). There is a self-referential element to her occupation as a novelist, particularly when the old man and the narrator have forgotten what novels are and question whether it is 'possible to write about something in a novel even if you've never experienced it' (p.195). The narrator's story reflects experiences and emotions from her own life, and brings her new perspectives, for example that she, like 'the woman in [her] novel[,] had also become trapped in a tight place' (p.132).

Ogawa emphasises the importance of storytelling to one's identity, as R describes the narrator's stories as existing on 'the surface of [her] soul' (p.214). The narrator feels that even though she has 'managed to finish the story ... [she's] still losing [herself]' (p.270), but for R it is important simply that 'the stories have begun to stir again' (p.245). For him, the act of her writing symbolises hope that the narrator will retain her sense of self, and her sense of humanity. When the books are burned by the citizens of the island, a woman who has not lost her memories cannot passively stand by and cries out to the citizens to stop what they are doing, insisting that 'no one can erase the stories!' (p.180). She is willing to sacrifice her own safety in an effort to make the citizens see the importance of storytelling.

When the narrator loses her body, she realises that stories are all that is left to her, emphasising that it is through storytelling that we leave our legacy. She wonders whether her story 'will remain after [she] disappear[s]' (p.270), finally able to see the importance of this, which R has been trying to convince her of all along.

### Key point

The old man's assertion that he 'would never want to do something as wasteful' (p.17) as reading a novel to the end might not be relatable for readers who enjoy savouring books and the experience of reading them. On a deeper level, it is ultimately a criticism of those who want to remain 'safe and sound, forever' (p.17). Ogawa implies that novels and stories should challenge us to take action.

# DIFFERENT INTERPRETATIONS

Different interpretations arise from different responses to a text. Over time, a text will evoke a wide range of responses from its readers, who may come from various social or cultural groups and live in very different places and historical periods. Responses by critics and reviewers can be published in newspapers, journals and books, both online and in print. They can also be expressed in discussions among readers in the media, classrooms, book groups and so on.

While there is no single correct reading or interpretation of a text, it is important to understand that an interpretation is more than a personal opinion – it is the justification of a point of view on the text. To present an interpretation of a text based on your point of view, you must use a logical argument and support it with relevant evidence from the text.

## Critical viewpoints

*The Memory Police* has received international recognition and praise and was shortlisted in 2020 for the International Booker Prize. Critical reviews of the novel seek to find allegorical meaning in Ogawa's dystopian world, making connections with old age and memory loss, physical disability and, more recently, the impacts of COVID-19.

Jia Tolentino, writing for *The New Yorker*, sees *The Memory Police* as an allegory for climate change, asserting that 'even when regularly confronted with the most concrete and urgent sort of reality—that we have less than a year and a half before the planet's climate is irreversibly headed toward catastrophe, for example—we tend, like the people in Ogawa's novel, to forget' (Tolentino 2019). Tolentino suggests that the novel's message is that issues such as climate change and fascism 'may be complex, but, if we fail to fully see them, this is at least partly because we have chosen to look away' (Tolentino 2019).

Comparatively, in the *Michigan Quarterly Review,* Julia Shiota proposes that Ogawa's argument is 'about historical revisionism' (Shiota 2021). She argues that the antagonists are not the Memory Police but the human beings who participate in 'invisible historical processes', and that Japan in particular 'has long struggled with acknowledging historical atrocities and its colonization of the Asian mainland and other countries in the Pacific' (Shiota 2021).

With regard to recent events, critics have found relevance for *The Memory Police* in terms of the isolation and fear caused by the global pandemic of COVID-19. Writing in March 2020, Joshua Keating stated that 'the outbreak feels more like *The Memory Police*—things disappearing from our lives before we can even process them' (Keating 2020). He draws parallels to losses that start off 'small and insignificant' and worries about 'which of thc things that disappeared this week are, like the objects in Ogawa's novel, never going to reappear' (Keating 2020). Sayantan Ghosh makes similar connections, seeing 'memory as protest' in Ogawa's novel, and suggesting that 'our memories are being permanently altered due to the social conditions wrought by the virus which has separated thousands of people from their friends and families' (Ghosh 2020).

Many critics praise Ogawa's prose, describing it as 'supple' and 'shifting' (Martin 2023), and 'direct' and 'understated' (Michaud 2019). But it is her ability to allow us new perspectives on our own humanity, and on our concerns about forgetting, death and the ending of everything, that has earned Ogawa her own legacy.

## Two interpretations

**_The Memory Police_ is a stark warning of the consequences of societal inaction.**

*The Memory Police* is an allegorical depiction of the dangers that arise from societal inaction and apathy. Regardless of whether readers view the allegory as representing climate change, totalitarian police states or social attitudes towards the elderly, Ogawa depicts the harm that is allowed to occur as a result of passive acceptance. This harm is both physical and emotional, and results in the maintenance of oppressive systems of power and the destruction of the world itself.

The most tangible impact of inaction in Ogawa's narrative is the physical harm suffered by individuals. As objects are disappeared, those who manage to retain their memories are hunted down and taken away by the Memory Police, who would then do 'anything they felt was necessary' (p.34). Ogawa implies that the narrator's mother was killed by the Memory Police, although 'nothing suspicious was found' (p.33). Even those who lose their memory suffer physical harm, as their inaction leads to increasing numbers of disappearances until even their 'entire bodies were gone' (p.270). This chilling image emphasises how, having adapted 'without too much inconvenience' (p.252) to the prior disappearances, their physical selves are violated.

This physical harm parallels a deeper psychological wound: the loss of identity. As objects vanish, along with them go personal and collective histories, erasing cultural identities. The societal erasure of music boxes and birds reveals that concepts such as art and the freedom of 'distant places' (p.187) are lost as well. The citizens cannot take comfort from the 'particularly soothing' sound of the music box (p.147) and cannot comprehend the enormity of the knowledge that is lost in the 'great mass of burning pages' (p.178) during the destruction of novels. Symbols of childhood nostalgia, like the *ramune*, the harmonica and the ferry rides, are gone, meaning that a whole generation has a much more limited experience of the world. This erasure extends to professions too, with many of the island's inhabitants defined by their jobs – the former hatmaker, the fishmonger, the new editor – and their occupational losses symbolise a loss of self. These erasures of cultural identity are facilitated by the complacency of the citizens, who are unable to recognise the significance of their losses until it is too late.

The Memory Police wield unchallenged power, taking advantage of, or perhaps creating, the disappearances, and manipulating societal norms and behaviours accordingly. The citizens make 'no attempt to escape their fate' (p.269) as they believe 'there's nothing too terrible about things disappearing—or forgetting about them' (p.54), and this obedience to the laws of the island allows the Memory Police to consolidate their power. The Memory Police justify their need to 'work in secret' (p.106), establishing rules that they 'determine' (p.105) with no consultation, causing the citizens to live in fear. Although originally protocol, soon there are no 'advance warnings' (p.64) of a visit from the police, and little 'kindness shown' (p.14) when they do visit. Ogawa's warning is clear: if you accept small and progressive inconveniences, it will allow authoritarian regimes to flourish, taking control without necessarily prioritising citizens' best interests. The passivity of the inhabitants of the island means that even those who resist seem to be resisting futilely, as by the end of the novel the Memory Police have such control that they have no need to 'go on hunting people who are no more than voices' (p.273).

This societal inaction makes way for the eventual collapse of the community and, by extension, the island itself. As the island gradually disappears 'under the weight of the snow' (p.273), Ogawa draws a clear parallel to real-world issues such as climate change, again highlighting the catastrophic consequences of such widespread apathy. The world 'is in ruins' (p.273) and although that provides some measure of freedom for R, for the majority of citizens this destruction comes at the cost of their own lives, as they are reduced to an 'unreliable and invisible voice' (p.273).

Ogawa's novel is a powerful argument against inaction and the acceptance of oppressive regimes. The disturbing reality of a society that passively accepts ever increasing losses is that individuals and communities will face physical harm and, eventually, death. Whether we read the destruction of the island as allegorical or not, complacency in the face of increasingly restrictive rules will result in a loss of our sense of safety, as it is difficult to ever feel at home or that you belong when you live in fear. Ogawa criticises the acceptance of the loss of collective history and culture, and urges us to question, resist and take action long before we are ever in danger of losing our bodies.

**_The Memory Police_ is concerned with individual responses to crisis.**

Ogawa's dystopian novel focuses on the impact, or lack of impact, that individuals have. In the face of increasing social change, characters in *The Memory Police* attempt courageous and individual acts of resistance, which are mostly ineffectual in their aims. While we might be led to rationally accept the horror of Ogawa's dystopia at a societal level, we do feel real empathy and compassion for individuals within the story.

Dystopian texts targeting young adults typically feature brave and resilient protagonists, who demonstrate the impact that one person acting against injustice can have. While there are characters who respond courageously to crisis in *The Memory Police*, Ogawa reveals the futility of doing so. When the novels disappear and the citizens of the island burn their books, a young woman protests this destruction of knowledge, screaming 'frantically' (p.179) and wanting them to 'put out the fire' (p.180). But she is quickly arrested by the Memory Police and although she 'tried to resist ... it was hopeless' (p.180). Even her final cry of warning that 'no one can erase the stories!' (p.180) is not comprehended by the citizens looking on, who simply sigh and '[turn] back to stare at the fire' (p.180). Similarly, individuals who risk their lives to hide those whose memories are intact seldom bestow long-term protection. They are usually found out by the Memory Police and 'forced ... into the covered back of one of the trucks' (p.155) along with those they sought to save. However well-intentioned or bravely characters may respond, they are unable to alter the grim reality of the world they inhabit.

Ogawa highlights individual acts of resistance throughout *The Memory Police* but suggests that these ultimately affect only the individuals themselves. The narrator's decision to 'go on writing ... in secret' (p.185) after the disappearance of the novels becomes an act of personal defiance rather than a large-scale rebellion. Even though she does manage to 'finish the story', she feels that she's 'still losing [herself]' (p.270). So, even though she has attempted to take control of her own soul, she is unsuccessful, leading us to question the value of this act of resistance. Likewise, the old man's decision to listen 'to the music box every day' (p.186) is an attempt to please someone else: R. It is an act of resistance as the music box has been disappeared, but it does not make the old man feel 'any different' or 'any stronger' (p.186). These examples demonstrate the insular nature of resistance within the novel – a resistance that seems to resonate and offer solace only on an individual level.

The aid provided in the face of crisis is similarly individualistic rather than collective. Citizens help one another on a one-to-one basis, offering food or taking in pets, as seen when the narrator fills 'the void in the [old woman's] basket' with celery (p.138) and 'began taking care of the dog that had belonged to the neighbors' (p.174). However, when the dog owners themselves were taken, not a single person raised a hand to save them. And even the support that is provided seems based on personal connection rather than on an underlying moral code. The narrator saves the old man when he is 'dying under that rubble' from the earthquake (p.236), but 'can't help' the woman in the street who is 'looking for someone who can hide [her]' (pp.171–2). Ogawa draws attention to the absence of community spirit, and the pointlessness of individual actions.

As readers, we can see the devastating consequences of the disappearances for the entire community, but the detachment and the complacency of the citizens who 'made no attempt to escape their fate' (p.269) make it difficult for us to empathise with them. We are left feeling almost as though they deserve it. This contrasts with the emotional response provoked by the death of the old man, the entrapment of the woman in the narrator's story, and the narrator's own disappearance. The narrator's final 'frail and hoarse' goodbye (p.274) elicits incredible sorrow from readers who have come to empathise with her desperate desire to cling to life and to 'exist as a memory' (p.270) if she must die. This mirrors our own responses and emotional investments when confronted with the plight of individuals in crisis, and suggests that although this might prompt us to act to help one person, it makes little difference to the overall crisis.

*The Memory Police* offers a stark assessment of the human capacity to confront systemic oppression, or indeed any crisis. Ogawa reveals the futility of individual actions, asserting that even when we feel empathy for others it is not enough to reverse the damages done to the world. We may feel in the moment as though individual acts of resistance have an impact, but the truth is that they have very little consequence at all.

# QUESTIONS & ANSWERS

This section focuses on your own analytical writing on the text, and gives you strategies for producing high-quality responses in your coursework and exam essays.

## Essay writing – an overview

An essay on a literary work is a formal and serious piece of writing that presents your point of view on the text, usually in response to a given topic. Your 'point of view' in an essay is your interpretation of the meaning of the text's language, structure, characters, situations and events, supported by detailed analysis of textual evidence.

### Analyse – don't summarise

In your essays it is important to avoid simply summarising what happens in a text.

- A **summary** is a description or paraphrase (retelling in different words) of the characters and events. For example: 'Macbeth has a horrifying vision of a dagger dripping with blood before he goes to murder King Duncan.'
- An **analysis** is an explanation of the real meaning or significance that lies 'beneath' the text's words (and images, for a film). For example: 'Macbeth's vision of a bloody dagger shows how deeply uneasy he is about the violent act he is contemplating, and conveys his sense that supernatural forces are impelling him to act.'

A limited amount of summary is sometimes necessary to let your reader know which part of the text you wish to discuss. However, always keep this to a minimum and follow it immediately with your analysis of what this part of the text is really telling us.

### Plan your essay

Carefully plan your essay so that you have a clear idea of what you are going to say. The plan ensures that your ideas flow logically, that your argument remains consistent and that you stay on the topic. An essay plan should be a list of **brief dot points** covering no more than half a page.

- Include your central argument or main contention – a concise statement of your overall response to the topic.
- Write three or four dot points for each paragraph, indicating the main idea and evidence/examples from the text. Note that in your essay you will need to expand on these points and analyse the evidence.

### Structure your essay

An essay is a complete, self-contained piece of writing. It has a clear beginning (the introduction), middle (several body paragraphs) and end (the last paragraph or conclusion). It must also have a central argument that runs throughout, linking each paragraph to form a coherent whole. See examples of introductions and conclusions in the 'Analysing a sample topic' and 'Sample answer' sections.

**The introduction establishes your overall response to the topic**. It includes your main contention and outlines the main evidence you will refer to in the course of the essay. Write your introduction *after* you have done a plan and *before* you write the rest of the essay.

**The body paragraphs argue your case** – they present evidence from the text and explain how this evidence supports your argument. Each body paragraph needs:

- a strong **topic sentence** (usually the first sentence) that states the main point being made in the paragraph
- **evidence** from the text, including some brief quotations
- **analysis** of the textual evidence, with **explanation** of its significance and how it supports your argument
- **links back to the topic** in one or more statements, usually towards the end of the paragraph.

Connect the body paragraphs so that your discussion flows smoothly. Use some linking words and phrases such as 'similarly' and 'on the other hand', though don't start every paragraph like this. Another strategy is to use a significant word from the last sentence of one paragraph in the first sentence of the next.

Use key terms from the topic – or synonyms for them – throughout, so the relevance of your discussion to the topic is always clear.

**The conclusion ties everything together and finishes the essay.** It includes strong statements that emphasise your central argument and provide a clear response to the topic.

Avoid simply restating the points made earlier in the essay – this will end on a very flat note and imply that you have run out of ideas and vocabulary. The conclusion should be a logical extension of what you have written, not just a repetition or summary of it. Writing an effective conclusion can be a challenge. Try using these tips:

- Start by linking back to the final sentence of the second-last paragraph, rather than leaping to your main contention straight away – this helps your writing to flow.
- Use synonyms and expressions with equivalent meanings to vary your vocabulary. This allows you to reinforce your line of argument without being repetitive.
- When planning your essay, think of one or two broad statements or observations about the text's wider meaning. These should be related to the topic and your overall argument. Keep them for the conclusion, since they will give you something 'new' to say but still follow logically from your discussion. The introduction will be focused on the topic, but the conclusion can present a wider view of the text.

## Essay topics

1 How does Ogawa use the character of R to explore the effects of isolation?

2 "Time is a great healer."
How does *The Memory Police* challenge or reinforce this notion?

3 How does the use of tone and language in *The Memory Police* contribute to its dystopian atmosphere?

4 "You forget, I'm the one who never loses anything."
'Ogawa suggests that those who remember experience greater suffering.' Discuss.

5 'The old man's complacency and acceptance represent the general population's reaction to an authoritarian regime.'
Do you agree?

6 '*The Memory Police* suggests that human relationships are the key to preserving memories in the face of systemic erasure.'
Do you agree?

7 "I suspect the only reason I've been able to go on writing is that I've had your heart by my side all along."
How does Ogawa demonstrate the importance of storytelling?

8 'Ogawa suggests that it is always women who have the most to lose.' To what extent do you agree?

9 How does Ogawa explore the idea of memory and its importance in human identity in *The Memory Police*?

10 'The characters in *The Memory Police* are not merely victims but also enablers of their oppressive society.' Do you agree?

## Vocabulary for writing on *The Memory Police*

***Allegory:*** A narrative that presents abstract or ethical ideas through characters, settings and events.

***Authoritarianism:*** A form of government characterised by a concentrated central power that places limitations on political freedoms.

***Censorship***: The restriction or banning of information, such as that in books, social media, the news etc., that is considered to be inappropriate, politically sensitive or a threat to security. *The Memory Police* symbolically depicts censorship, a tool often used by oppressive regimes, through the erasure of objects and memories.

***Dystopia:*** An imagined world where there is great suffering or inequity.

***Foil***: A character whose qualities are designed to conflict with another character, usually the protagonist, in order to highlight certain traits and values in the latter. In *The Memory Police*, R acts as a foil to the narrator, as he is one of the few who can remember the disappeared objects, highlighting the narrator's losses.

***Foreshadowing:*** A narrative device that hints at upcoming events; used to build suspense or prepare the reader for eventual outcomes.

***Imagery:*** Language used by writers to create images in the mind of the reader, often appealing to our senses.

***Motif***: A repeated symbol or idea throughout a text. For example, snow is a motif in *The Memory Police*.

***Narrative voice:*** The perspective or persona that is telling the story. *The Memory Police* is told using a first-person narrative voice, from the point of view of an unnamed female novelist.

***Symbol:*** Something that represents or stands for something else. Often, a symbol is an object that represents something abstract.

***Tone:*** The specific manner of expression in writing that reflects the writer's attitude towards the subject and the audience.

## Analysing a sample topic

**'The characters in *The Memory Police* are not merely victims but also enablers of their oppressive society.' Do you agree?**

To respond to this topic, begin by brainstorming a list of characters in *The Memory Police*. Consider the main ones such as the narrator or the woman in the her novel, as well as less obvious characters such as Professor Inui. Then consider your contention. You might argue that although the characters suffer, through their complacency they enable the Memory Police to take control. You might entirely disagree, contending that the characters are victims with no power or agency. You could also think about individual characters: R, for example, as he is hiding in the secret room, is not able to take action and therefore might be considered merely a victim. The old man, on the other hand, has had a lifetime to observe the effects of the disappearances and still has made no attempt at resisting – perhaps his inaction has contributed to the oppressive society he lives in.

Make sure that you think about the different elements of the oppressive society as you are planning your essay. Of course, you will write about the role of the Memory Police, but think about the effect of the disappearances and other features of this world, such as the food shortages and the relentless winter. For each of them, consider whether characters have enabled that element, or whether they are simply victims of it.

### Sample introduction

Yōko Ogawa's dystopian novel *The Memory Police* depicts a chilling authoritarian regime. When an object disappears, the titular Memory Police enforce the disappearance, ensuring any remnants or records of the object are destroyed, and arresting anyone who is able to retain their memory of it. The characters in the novel suffer within this culture of fear to varying degrees, experiencing physical and social isolation and eventually real bodily harm. But for most of the inhabitants of the island, their complacency and lack of action enables the Memory Police to wield power and continue to maintain control.

### Body paragraph outline

**Paragraph 1:** In any oppressive society, there are those who benefit from the oppression and enable it to continue.

- The Memory Police receive comforts the other inhabitants of the island are not afforded, such as a stable supply of food (p.225), and maintain a luxurious way of life – their headquarters are decorated with 'an elaborate elevator' and 'an enormous chandelier' (p.102), all symbols of their wealth and power.
- The frequent descriptions of the Memory Police as 'efficient' (p.13) and 'violent' (p.12) suggest that they are machine-like in their carrying out of tasks, and therefore unable to be reasoned with.
- The typing teacher in the narrator's novel clearly relishes the power he has over the woman in the clock tower. He demonstrates his oppression physically: 'closing his hand ... tightly around [the woman's] throat' (p.131) and forcing her into 'strangely shaped garments' (p.165).
- The typing teacher is a serial abuser, who benefits from the silence of the young women he teaches and then imprisons. He is 'glad' to be 'able to erase' the voice of the woman (p.132) and enjoys telling her that he will 'capture' the voice of another young girl 'until it's completely absorbed and the keys no longer move' (p.265).

**Paragraph 2:** *The Memory Police* depicts characters who are, in spite of their desire for agency, purely victims of their patriarchal and violent society.

- The narrator's mother makes every effort to resist the disappearances, hiding disappeared objects in her sculptures and drawers and giving some to the Inuis for safekeeping (p.36). In spite of this, she is targeted by the Memory Police and has 'no obvious reason to refuse' their summons (p.33). Ogawa implies that she is killed by the police, as her body was returned 'with her death certificate' (p.33).
- The woman in the narrator's novel is trapped with no means of escape. Her story, although it includes elements of magical realism, is soberingly recognisable. She is a victim of abuse, and is told she has 'no need to talk, no need to utter a single word' (p.131).
- The mountain of typewriters 'stacked as high as [the woman's] head' (p.128) symbolises all the women who have been subjected to the typing teacher's silencing and abuse.

**Paragraph 3:** Ogawa suggests that many characters enable their own suffering through their complacency and acceptance.

- The old man maintains a positive attitude even in the face of the growing number of disappearances. His constant refrain of 'that's nothing for you to worry yourself over' (p.51) is naively ignorant, and ultimately allows the Memory Police to continue carrying out their violence.
- The old man's attitude reflects the perspective of the society as a whole. Even when people begin to lose their limbs, they believe that they understand 'the nature of the disappearances' and know 'the best way to deal with them' (p.269).
- Ogawa uses metaphor to emphasise the irony of the citizens' inaction. The narrator tells Don, 'If I'd realized sooner what was happening, we might have saved him' (p.255). This is a clear call to action: if you don't act on the things that matter, it will be too late.
- Unlike the characters in the narrator's novel, the inhabitants of the island have their voices until their final moment of existence. Voices symbolise identity and agency and Ogawa suggests here that the victims of this regime could have spoken out against their oppression right until the end, but chose not to.

**Paragraph 4:** The novel endorses characters who resist oppression in spite of their own victimisation, but suggests that this resistance is usually futile.

- R speaks out against the oppressive system he is trapped in, urging the narrator and the old man to hold the 'forgotten objects in [their] hands' (p.146). He gives up his home and his life with his wife and unborn child in order to protect them as well as himself. However, at the end of the novel 'the outside world is in ruins' (p.273) and it is not clear if any of it will have been worth it.

- The narrator also resists the control of the Memory Police. She continues to write when the novels have been disappeared, and she seems to genuinely question the value of the disappearances, unlike others in her community. But the loss of her memories makes it difficult for her to act with any real power.
- There are characters in the novel who risk their safety to hide those who remember, but these efforts seem futile as the Memory Police hunt them down and take them away. Even though 'there must be more than one boatload of people trying to get off the island' (p.115), Ogawa suggests that the likely consequence for these escapees is drowning.

### Sample conclusion

Although there are obviously those who perpetuate the violence and oppression of the novel's police state, most characters are indeed victims of their authoritarian society. However, their passivity and resignation to this reality contribute to its continuation. We are positioned to sympathise with victims who have no agency or power to resist the forces that constrain them, and are equally led to condemn characters who facilitate their own oppression. Ogawa makes it clear that while we have the human capacity to endure and resist oppression, our efforts will be futile if we act alone.

# SAMPLE ANSWER

**How does Ogawa use the character of R to explore the effects of isolation?**

Yōko Ogawa's novel *The Memory Police* is allegorical in its representation of an authoritarian police state, but ultimately the text is concerned with individuals and the way they can offer new perspectives on our own humanity. The character of R is unique, as he is able to remember the objects that everyone else forgets. This makes him a target for the Memory Police, and his concealment in the narrator's hidden room both saves him and damages him irreparably. While the physical effects of isolation are the most obvious early on, it is his loss of connection and sense of reality that reveals the true horrors of his secret existence.

Ogawa describes the physical deterioration of R in order to tangibly represent the debilitating effects of isolation. R is described as 'large', and in the 'airless, soundproof, narrow space' of the hidden room, he is often depicted as 'hunched' or with 'his back ... bent as though in prayer'. The narrator feels she can see 'his body blurring, his blood thinning, his muscles withering' every time she sees him, emphasising the physical toll of his seclusion. Without any access to the world beyond his hidden room, R grows 'pale' and 'los[es] weight'. The narrator suggests that R's body is ridding itself 'of everything that was superfluous' but this seems an optimistic view for the brutally physical reduction of R's self. Although Ogawa posits that this bodily decay is a trade-off for his memories, she also implies that there is a danger that R will eventually 'fade away'.

R's characterisation reveals the loss of identity that can occur as a result of isolation. To go into hiding, R must part with his pregnant wife. Initially unwilling, he ultimately assents, hoping he will one day 'be reunited with her and [their] baby'. But having to give up his role as husband and father means he loses a crucial part of his identity. When his son is born, 'photographs have already disappeared', and R must make do with 'a portrait of a baby with its eyes closed'. Left without even a proper visual aid, R has lost any real chance of fatherhood. We are not invited to judge or condemn R for his choice to sleep with the narrator, but it is yet another indication of what he has lost. His only chance for connection is with the narrator and it is possible that they both see it as necessary for their own survival, that 'in order to protect each other, [they] had simply taken refuge in the only safe place left to [them]'.

Ogawa's exploration of the effects of isolation culminates in the impact on R's sense of reality. Even in the early days of his isolation, R feels so disconnected from the world that he is convinced he is living 'in a cave, suspended in the middle of nothingness'. By the end of the novel, he proposes that both he and the narrator stay in the hidden room, because they'll be 'safe' and 'protected' with 'all the things that were hidden in the sculptures'. Both the reader and the narrator know that this is 'impossible', not least because they would have no way of obtaining food. This irrational perspective on the world extends somewhat to a shift in R's personality. The longer he remains isolated, the more possessive he seems to be of the narrator. He tells her that he will 'keep [her] safe' in his 'secret room'. And, where once he resisted the disappearances, by the time the narrator has begun losing body parts, R assures her 'there's nothing to cry about', mimicking the complacency and acceptance of the other inhabitants of the island. Ogawa encourages us to distrust these assurances, and to see that this shift in attitude and behaviour is a result of his prolonged isolation, and his lack of human connection.

Ogawa's characterisation of R allows her to illuminate the chilling effects of isolation. In many ways, R is the most relatable character for readers as, like him, we retain all our memories of the things the citizens of the island have forgotten. This means that we vicariously experience R's isolation and appreciate the anguish and bewilderment caused by such a profound disconnection from society. R reflects the human condition under severe isolation, highlighting the inherent need for connection and interaction that defines us as social beings.

# REFERENCES & READING


## Text

Ogawa, Y 2020, *The Memory Police* (Snyder S trans), Penguin Random House, London. First published in 1994.

## Books and journal articles

Frank, A 1993, *The Diary of a Young Girl*, Bantam Books, New York. First published in 1947.

Iris, C 2012, *The Rape of Nanking: The Forgotten Holocaust of World War II*, Basic Books, New York. First published in 1997.

## Websites

Adams, G 2022, 'Dystopian fiction: comforting or terrifying?', *Cherwell*, 15 February, https://cherwell.org/2022/02/15/dystopian-fiction-comforting-or-terrifying/

Aharony, M 2010, 'Hannah Arendt and the Idea of Total Domination', *Holocaust and Genocide Studies*, vol. 24, no. 2, pp.193–224.

Atchison, A & Shames, S 2020, 'Are we living in a dystopia?', *The Conversation*, 29 April, https://theconversation.com/are-we-living-in-a-dystopia-136908

Ghosh, S 2020, 'Yoko Ogawa's *The Memory Police* is a terrifying chronicle of a totalitarian regime, examining remembrance as protest', *Firstpost*, 25 August, https://www.firstpost.com/art-and-culture/Yoko-ogawas-the-memory-police-is-a-terrifying-chronicle-of-a-totalitarian-regime-examining-remembrance-as-protest-8723391.html

Keating, J 2020, 'The Dystopian Novel for the Social Distancing Era', *Slate*, 20 March, https://slate.com/culture/2020/03/memory-police-ogawa-coronavirus-social-distancing.html

Kellerman, S & O'Conner PT 2013, 'A disappearing act', *Grammarphobia*, 12 August, https://www.grammarphobia.com/blog/2013/08/disappear.html

Kimie, I 2020, 'Writer Ogawa Yōko's Stories of Memory and Loss', *Nippon Communications Foundation*, 27 March, https://www.nippon.com/en/people/bg900133/writer-ogawa-yoko's-stories-of-memory-and-loss.html cx_recs_click=true

Macmillan Publishers 2023, *Yoko Ogawa*, Macmillan Publishers, https://us.macmillan.com/author/yokoogawa

Margolis, E 2020, 'The Titanic Literary Accomplishment of Yoko Ogawa', *Metropolis*, 12 February, https://metropolisjapan.com/yoko-ogawa-memory-police

Martin, T 2023, 'The Booker Prize guide to ... dystopian fiction', *Booker Prize Foundation*, 27 January, https://thebookerprizes.com/the-booker-library/features/the-booker-prize-guide-to-dystopian-fiction

Michaud, J 2019, 'In "The Memory Police," an authoritarian government tries to erase the past', *The Washington Post*, 15 August, https://www.washingtonpost.com/entertainment/books/in-the-memory-police-an-authoritarian-government-tries-to-erase-the-past/2019/08/15/9cc3a7ea-be9a-11e9-b873-63ace636af08_story.html

Rich, M 2019, 'Yoko Ogawa Conjures Spirits in Hiding: "I Just Peeked Into Their World and Took Notes"', *The New York Times*, 12 August, https://www.nytimes.com/2019/08/12/books/yoko-ogawa-memory-police.html

shelfmedia 2020, 'Interview: Stephen Snyder. Translator for The Memory Police by Yoko Ogawa', shelfmedia group, October 4, https://shelfmediagroup.com/interview/interview-stephen-snyder-translator-for-the-memory-police-by-yoko-ogawa

Shiota, J 2021, 'Yoko Ogawa's The Memory Police and the Dangers of Forgetting', *Michigan Quarterly Review*, July, https://sites.lsa.umich.edu/mqr/2021/07/Yoko-ogawas-the-memory-police-and-the-dangers-of-forgetting

Tolentino, J 2019, 'How "The Memory Police" makes you see', *The New Yorker*, 6 November, https://www.newyorker.com/books/under-review/how-the-memory-police-makes-you-see

The Weiner Holocaust Library (n.d.), *Resistance: Hiding*, The Holocaust Explained, https://www.theholocaustexplained.org/resistance-responses-collaboration/resistance/hiding